Lisa St Aubin de Terán's first [illegible] won the Somerset Maugham A[illegible] *The Slow Train to Milan*, whic[illegible]lyn Rhys Prize. She has written six o[illegible]ovels, poetry, short stories and four memoirs, including the bestselling *The Hacienda*.

elements of Italy

EDITED AND INTRODUCED BY

Lisa St Aubin de Terán

Virago

A *Virago* Book

Published by Virago Press 2002
Reprinted 2003
First published by Virago Press 2001

This collection and introduction copyright © Lisa St Aubin de Terán 2001

Copyright acknowledgements on pp. v–viii constitute
an extension of this copyright page

The publisher extends grateful thanks to Jennifer Hicks
for invaluable editorial research and assistance

The moral right of the editor has been asserted.

A CIP catalogue record for this book
is available from the British Library.

ISBN 1 86049 924 4

Typeset in Garamond by M Rules
Printed and bound in Great Britain by
Clays Ltd, St Ives plc

Virago
An imprint of
Time Warner Books UK
Brettenham House
Lancaster Place
London WC2E 7EN

www.virago.co.uk

ACKNOWLEDGEMENTS

The publishers gratefully acknowledge the following for permission to reprint copyright material:

From *Sea and Sardinia* and *Etruscan Places* by D.H. Lawrence, Laurence Pollinger Ltd and the Estate of Frieda Lawrence Ravagli; from *Death in Venice* by Thomas Mann, published by Martin Secker & Warburg/Minerva, from *Circles of Hell* by Eric Morris, published by Hutchinson, from *Italian Journeys* by Jonathan Keates, published by William Heinemann, from *Standing in the Sun* by Antony Bailey, published by Sinclair-Stevenson, from *Excellent Cadavers* by Alexander Stille, published by Vintage, from *Men Without Women* by Ernest Hemingway, published by Arrow, all reprinted by permission of The Random House Group Ltd; from *Death in Rome* by Wolfgang Koeppen, translated by Michael Hoffman (Hamish Hamilton, 1992) copyright © Wolfgang Koeppen 1954, translation copyright © Michael Hoffman 1992, from *A Capote Reader* by Truman Capote (Hamish Hamilton, 1987) copyright © Alan U. Schwartz, 1987, from *The New Italians* by Charles Richards (Michael Joseph, 1994) copyright © Charles Richards 1994, from *Watermark* by Joseph Brodsky (Hamish Hamilton, 1996) copyright © the Estate of Joseph Brodsky,

Not only have innumerable writers written about Italy, innumerable writers have pleaded the sheer numbers of those who wrote before as a deterrent to saying anything more about her. Just as Henry James wrote of Venice: '. . . I am not sure there is not a certain impudence in pretending to add anything to it . . .' and then went on like so many others to wax lyrical, so, in time-honoured fashion, I draw attention to the hundreds of tomes already published on the subject and proceed to add another, sheltering under James's influential wing when he states: '. . . I hold any writer sufficiently justified who is himself in love with his theme.'

My love affair with Italy began when I was a child of eight and first read Byron's letters. While still at school, I married a stranger because he kept saying 'Let's go to Italy.' I have followed in Byron's footsteps, lived and loved here for the longest part of my life. I can almost say with Browning:

> *Open my heart and you will see*
> *Graved inside of it, 'Italy'*

Because of the sheer volume of material and because of the intense nature of much of it, I have chosen the Elements of Italy to sift and sort the mountains of matter. My four categories are the four classical elements of earth, water, fire and air: four channels to convey the essence of Italy; what it is about, what it looks like, smells like, sounds and tastes like. Unlike in other anthologies, though, I have attempted to show some of the elements that have shaped Italy beyond the realms of the aesthetic.

This is a country full of passion, and a country which foreigners feel passionate about. Stendhal concluded: 'The charm of Italy is akin to that of being in love.'

I will try and show the lover and the beloved: to see some of the things engraved on Italian hearts. Beautiful, tyrannical landscapes, poverty, power and politics, the mass emigration of nine million, the intense love of family, the pride of place, the celebration of food (captured first and best by Elizabeth David), the boundless generosity, brilliance and wit of a people who spill art through their fingertips every day in the mimicry and gestures of their speech like a thousand side shows of the *Commedia dell' Arte*.

So, under the heading of 'Fire', the Mafia, revolution and war stand side by side with a landscape of erupting volcanoes and Leonardo da Vinci's observations of the sun.

Chaos and corruption are two components of Italian life so present they cannot be ignored. Visitors love Italy despite its chaos; they are often so bowled over by the other elements that they fail to be aware of the corruption. Those who detect the corruption often fail to be aware of an underlying purity in most Italians who have survived and suffered both. Only a tiny minority have caused this corruption. I find the way most Italians have struggled for air under the miasma of crime heroic. And how many of us see under the facade of chaos a deep-rooted love of order? Here is a country that can function without a government; it often has done since the war! As to the Mafia, it is only in the last eight years that any real under-standing of it has come about. Most of the books on this subject have appeared post-'96. It has been my privilege as an editor to collect extracts from such extraordinary books as Alexander Stille's *Excellent Cadavers* and Peter Robb's *Midnight in Sicily*. Something crucial happened in Italy with the death of Judge Falcone in May 1992: a renaissance of hope. The tree that grows outside the murdered judge's Palermo apartment has become a shrine, full of messages, among them: 'They closed your eyes but you have opened ours.'

The turnstile into Italy has clicked continually for centuries. Most visitors pass anonymously; some, like Shelley and Keats, left not only their myths and words, but died here. Lord Byron loved here and continues to draw romantics in his wake like a magnet. Stendhal understood his rapture, a state many others have felt bound to record. Some, like Vita Sackville-West, have grown drunk on it and tried to own its volatile bouquet. Heinrich Heine noted that 'simply letting yourself live is beau-tiful in Italy'.

And yet, Italians themselves love their country more than any foreigner ever can because it is inside them in a way that few countries are to such a degree. This is a country where labour-ers *do* hum Verdi, quote Dante and find their lunch delicious. As Luigi Barzini points out:

Not many Italians willingly travel abroad in any direction, north, south, east or west. They always feel more or less exiled and unhappy in alien lands, and honestly believe the attractions of their homeland to be most satisfying. They are the first victims of the famous charm of Italy, never satiated with her sights, climate, food, music and life. Familiarity never breeds contempt in them. Neapolitans, for instance, after many thousand years, still gaze with the same rapture on their landscape, eat *spaghetti alle vongole* as if they had never tasted them before, and compose endless songs dedicated to the immortal beauty of their women and their bay.

I am often asked why I have chosen to live in Italy (I have been here for seventeen years now), and my answers include the Italians' love of art, the beauty of both landscape and architecture, and the people's love of life and generosity of spirit.

It was this generosity that took in and hid Allied soldiers during the war: the soldiers, if caught, risked prisoner-of-war camps, their hosts risked a death penalty for harbouring them. *Love and War in the Apennines* by Eric Newby (who went on to marry his protectress) tells such a tale. Norman Lewis's tragi-comic account of Naples '44 is but one of the many classics included here.

Something happens in Italy: people cross into new emotional fields. In Florence, every year, a handful of tourists are treated for what is known medically as 'Stendhal's Syndrome' – being overwhelmed by an excess of beauty. In Rome, it is easier to see how a poet like Goethe could find 'all the dreams of my youth I now behold realised before me' than to explain how Edward Gibbon with his temper 'not very susceptible of enthusiasm' was so swept off his feet. A lyrical, rhapsodic radiance seems to envelop the coolest and most rational of beings.

There is an overlapping of elements everywhere, a crossing of strands that makes for a weave at once distinctive and volatile. Attempts to capture this essence fray at the edges, roaming through the crass to the sentimental cliché en route. But there is so much, and out of that amount are gems as pure as the SSI, the pure white marble from Carrara known as *statuario* which has been carved by sculptors from Michelangelo to Mitoraj.

In *The Leopard* Guiseppe di Lampedusa writes of the Salina family who 'for centuries had been incapable even of adding up their own expenditure and subtracting their own debts'. He describes a family benign and decadent, swallowed up by their own traditions to the exclusion of all else. *The Leopard* is the story of a prince and one of the great works of literature this century. Another entirely different masterpiece is the incantatory *Fontamara* written by the communist Ignazio Silone in exile in Switzerland. It tells the story of peasants in his native village where:

> *God is at the head of everything. He commands*
> *everything. Everyone knows that.*
> *Then there is Prince Torlonia, ruler of the earth.*
> *Then comes the prince's guards.*
> *Then come his guards' dogs.*
> *Then nothing.*
> *Then more nothing.*
> *Then come all the peasants.*
> *That's all.*

The Sicilian palaces and estates of the prince fall under the category of 'Earth', while under the heading of 'Air' there are wind, angels, music, sky, wings and all manner of flying. Leonardo da Vinci, in his notebooks, manages to link and weave all of these.

At Etna and Versuvius fire erupts out of the earth, in Venice a city is built on water. Some of the surreal qualities of Venice are like a metaphor for Italy itself, a conscious layering of artifice and an unconscious laying down of truths. This is the country that made a horse a senator, the country that can combine tyranny with wit. When Hitler came to visit Rome in 1938, Mussolini transformed its slums by facing them with cardboard like film sets, prompting Trilussa's epigram: '*Roma di travertino, refatta de cartone, saluta l'imbianchino, suo prossimo padrone.*' (Rome of travertine, re-made with cardboard, greets the house painter who will be her next master.) The illusion worked, and Hitler was suitably impressed. One of my favourites is the Emperor Vespasian (who invented the public lavatory, called to this day a *vespasiano*) who died in A.D. 79 saying, 'Oh dear, I must be turning into a god.'

When Dante wrote his *Divine Comedy* he could not have known what hordes of foreigners would come to his country and find it divine. This stilettoed boot, set in two seas, seems to have walked across more hearts than any other country. Charles Fitzroy points out 'the most extraordinary aspect of Italian culture is its sheer variety . . . Italy today contains all the elements that so excited our ancestors . . .'

There is intoxication, delirium, a forgiveness of all that is indifferent and an adulation of 'the magic of Italy'. What Joseph Addison said in the eighteenth century still holds true today:

There is certainly no place in the world where a man may travel with greater pleasure and advantage than in Italy. One finds something more particular in the face of the country, and more astonishing in the works of nature, than can be met with in any other part of Europe. It is the great school of music and painting, and contains in it all the noblest productions of sculpture and architecture, both ancient and modern.

And with twenty-eight governments since 1945 it is fair to say, as Addison did: 'No other country in the world has such a variety of governments that are so different in their constitutions . . .'

At Cassino, in 1944, the Allies suffered one crushing defeat after another with slaughterous casualties. It was one of the worst moments of the war for them, and yet that strange miracle of place occurs even at that time of massacre. Major the Lord Tweedsmuir tells how he went to find Oliver Leese and report on the situation: 'When I saw Oliver he was in a field of cornflowers. He put out a hand to bring me to a halt and said, "Stop!" before I had a chance to tell him anything. He said, "Let's pick some cornflowers." Then he said, "Right. Now tell me about the casualties."'

Devastation meets *Room with a View* as even inside the circles of hell, men were touched by beauty.

No part of the watery element will raise itself or make itself more distant from the common centre except by violence. No violence is lasting.

LEONARDO DA VINCI

Despite Goethe's claim that to have seen Italy without seeing Sicily is not to have seen Italy at all, there has long been a divide between north and south and a frontier of poverty that forced millions of southerners to emigrate (mostly to America). Carlo Levi wrote: 'No one has come to this land except as an enemy, a conqueror, or a visitor devoid of understanding . . . no message, human or divine, has reached this stubborn poverty.'

Even Christ, it is said, stopped at Eboli. Norman Douglas lived among southern Italians for thirty years and wrote in *Old Calabria* during the peak period of the exodus: 'Ages of oppression and disrule has passed over their heads, sun and rain with all their caprice have been kinder friends to them than their earthly masters.'

In much of Italy, prosperity has taken over from poverty. Luigi Barzini in his *The Italians* tells us: 'Italy is still a country of limitless opportunities. It offers stage settings for all kinds of adventures, licit or illicit loves, the study of art, the experiences of pathos, the weaving of intrigues. It can be gay, tragic, mad, pastoral, archaic, modern or simply *dolce*.'

Truths and observations accumulate like tesserae in a Roman mosaic, building up a picture from fragments. So W.H. Auden adds his bit in the introduction to a new edition of Goethe's *Italian Journey* when he asks: 'Is there any other country in Europe where the character of the people seems to have been so little affected by political and technological change?'

Some things have changed though. In the nineteenth century, Leopardi asserted that: 'Italians do not write or think about their customs, as if they thought such studies were not useful to them.' Since then, there have been such remarkable writers as Silone, Lampedusa, Carlo and Primo Levi, each of whom has distilled the essence of their customs – of north and south – and made great works of literature from the microcosm they have observed and analysed.

Primo Levi was an Italian Jewish chemist who survived Auschwitz. Sometimes he saw life through chemical elements, as in *The Periodic Table*, an entire book of elements, each one relating in some way to the author.

Under the heading of 'Water', whether it is on the banks of the great river of life, or flowing with it, the extracts go from Verga's fishing village in *I Malavoglia*, to Byron in Venice gliding down the canals and Henry James in the Serenissima marvelling at the beauty of his surroundings, to Thomas Mann brooding on death and Lord Nelson saving the day in Naples.

And, just as the elements overlap, so do the entries here. So Byron travels from Venice to Ravenna in the pursuit of love, Shelley travels the same road to see him. Dickens is regaled with tales of Bryon, Turner travels through Italy seeing it through Shelley's eyes and verse, Keats goes to Rome to die by the Spanish Steps, Shelley is drowned with a copy of Keats's poetry in his pocket. Augustus Hare visits Rome and visits the two poets' graves. Truman Capote moves to Ischia, then Sicily; Cecil Beaton goes to visit him and events are told from both sides.

I have also included extracts of Italy seen by contemporary Italian writers, several of whom are unknown outside of Italy, for instance Marco Rufino evoking passion and place in his novel *Under a Distant Sky* (*Sotto un Cielo Lontano*). If I have not included yet more writers, it is through the dictatorship of space. An anthology of Italy could be almost limitless. But if writing about Italy has to stop somewhere, it can do no better than to finish with the words of Stendhal. On class, he says: 'A marquise of the highest nobility may be the friend of a simple drawing teacher . . . Vanity is but one of the passions, far from being the ruling one . . . A man living on an income of fifteen hundred francs speaks to a man who has an income of six millions simply as he would to an equal. This would be thought incredible in England.'

And lastly:

'It is their manners as a whole, their natural ways, *bonhomie*, the great art of being happy which is here practised with this added charm, that the good people do not know that it is an art, the most difficult of all.'

LISA ST AUBIN DE TERÁN

Morra

EARTH

When Dame Fortune pales
Throw yourself upon the earth
And start collecting snails.

ITALIAN PROVERB

Earth suitable for general use.
The earth to be generally used ought to be that of which bricks
are made mixed with ox-dung or clippings of woollen cloth.

  From *The Notebooks of Leonardo da Vinci*, ed. IRMA A. RICHTER

The incomparable wrought fusion, fusion of human history
and moral passion with the elements of earth and air, of colour,
composition and form; that constitute her appeal and give it
supreme heroic grace.

HENRY JAMES

A man who has never been to Italy is always conscious of an
inferiority . . . the grand object of travelling is to see the shores
of the Mediterranean.

DR JOHNSON

Italy seemed to me to be Nature's Darling, and the Eldest Sister
of all other countryes.

RICHARD LASSELS

It is their manners as a whole, their natural ways, bonhomie, the great art of being happy which is here practised with this added charm, that the good people do not know that it is an art, the most difficult of all.   STENDHAL

MILAN

Milan has seemed prosaic and winterish as if it were on the wrong side of the Alps.

HENRY JAMES

Bathed in the silver radiance of moonlight, Milan Cathedral is a thing of such ravishing beauty that all the world cannot contain its equal.

PERCY BYSSHE SHELLEY

GENOA

Their men are as devoid of faith, and their women of shame, as their hills are of wood, and their sea of fishes.

JOSEPH ADDISON

The peculiar joys of Italy in the perfumes of orange, citron, and jassmine flowers.

JOHN EVELYN

Genoa makes a dazzling appearance when viewed from the sea, rising like an amphitheatre in a circular form.

TOBIAS SMOLLETT

FLORENCE

Florence is nothing better than a vast museum full of foreign tourists,

STENDHAL

I cannot tell why this city should be termed beautiful as it were by privilege. Beautiful it is, but no more so than Bologna, and little more than Ferrara, while it falls far short of Venice.

MICHEL DE MONTAIGNE

I have done nothing but slip out of my domino (black and white masked costume) into bed, and out of my bed into my domino. The end of the Carnival is frantic, bacchanalian; all the morn one makes parties in masque to the shops and coffee-houses, and all the evening to the operas and balls. Then I have danced, good gods! how I have danced!

HORACE WALPOLE

The expatriates took a passionate interest in Italian politics and, inspired with revolutionary fervour and romantic views of the Rights of the Common Man, fervently supported the Risorgimento. Many of them, particularly writers, retired to the wooded hills surrounding Florence, where they could escape from the stifling summer heat in the city. Fiesole, with its beautiful views of the Duomo and the city in the bowl below, became the most fashionable retreat.

A few eccentrics helped to enliven the social scene: Walter Savage Landor, one of the first to collect Florentine Primitives, lived in the palazzo Medici for years, quarrelling with everyone and even, on occasion, beating up his carpenters. And the novelist Ouida drove around in a silk-lined victoria, proclaimed herself the greatest author of all time and scandalised society with her passions for eligible young men.

From 1865 to 1870 Florence was the capital of Italy and, for a brief moment, it seemed as though the city would bestride the world stage once more. The old ghetto was swept away and a façade finally put on the Duomo, but, as the tide of history swept on to Rome, it soon lapsed back to its status as the most popular tourist site in Italy. With its well-furnished apartments, hard-working population and lack of beggars, Florence was the acceptable face of Italy for the well-heeled middle classes and, in contrast with the male-dominated Grand Tour, vast numbers of women, thirsting for culture, descended on the city. The Americans, just as enthusiastic as their British contemporaries, compared the busy, intellectual life of Florence to that of Boston.

At the end of the nineteenth century Henry James was one of those to lead the reaction against the earnestness of these tourists, particularly Ruskin. 'I had really been enjoying the good old city of Florence,' he wrote in *Italian Hours*, 'but I now learned from Mr Ruskin that this was a scandalous waste of charity. I should have worn a face a yard long.'

They say that Julius Caesar himself was responsible for founding Florence, and that after Fiesole had been attacked and captured he determined in company with several other Roman nobles to build a city in which each one of them would undertake the construction of one of these notable edifices.

One of Caesar's first-ranking and bravest officers was called Fiorino and came from Cellini, a village about two miles away from Monte Fiasconi. This Fiorino decided to have his quarters under the hill of Fiesole, where Florence is today, because it would be convenient for the troops to be stationed near the River Arno. All the soldiers and other people connected with this captain acquired the habit of saying when they went to pay him a visit: 'Let's go along to Fiorenze.'

They said this because Fiorino, as I mentioned before, was the captain's name, and also because the natural fertility of the soil encouraged an abundant growth of flowers in the place where he had his camp. So Caesar decided to call the new city Florence (Fiorenze), as it was a very beautiful name and very apposite, and it seemed, with its suggestion of flowers, to make a good omen: and besides that he wanted to show what a high regard he had for his courageous captain, especially as he himself had raised Fiorino from a very humble rank and was responsible for his greatness.

From *Autobiography*, BENVENUTO CELLINI

It was their lovely ways, far more than their monuments of history and art, that made return to the Florentines delightful.

WILLIAM DEAN HOWELLS

Along the Arno towards Florence and a picturesque landscape with the old tow-path curving ahead of us, the ragged fishermen fishing in the river from the grassy banks or from frail green-and-brown skiffs, the woodchoppers hewing the trees from the opposite mountain side, the fleet of white ducks paddling and drifting with the current; and loveliest, a group of thatched cottages clustering together to form a large farm building orange and pink and bird's-egg blue, the color of the walls reflected in the river: gray-blue smoke ascending through gray stillness.

Towards evening Brozzi, and here, exhausted, hired a two-wheeled cart and jogged and jounced into Firenze by night, warming our hands over a brown earthenware pot filled with red ashes.

From *Shadows of the Sun*, HARRY CROSBY

SIENA

Very dreamy, and fantastic, and most interesting.

CHARLES DICKENS

Next he asked him how the man I had hurled the stone at was getting on. Pierantonio said that he was very ill and would get even worse, as he knew that I was back in Rome and had sworn that he would die, just to get even with me. The Cardinal roared with laughter at this and said: 'He couldn't find a better way of making us quite sure that he was born in Siena.'

BENVENUTO CELLINI

Siena's almost perfect medieval appearance, now regarded as one of the most delightful sights in Italy, was, for centuries, almost completely ignored. An exception was Fynes Moryson, one of the earliest foreigners to visit the city, who wrote, 'There is no place to live in through all Italy than the state of Florence, and more specially the sweet City of Sienna,' but his advice went unheeded. Most Grand Tourists, stopping overnight en route for Rome, did no more than praise it for its beneficial climate and the purity of the Italian spoken here. Boswell stayed for several weeks in 1765, but confessed, 'I have been a week in Siena and have not as yet seen any *meraviglia* (sights), as the Italians say . . . because I have been so busy with women that I have felt no curiosity about inanimate objects.'

He managed to carry on two affairs simultaneously at a fast and furious pace. On 10 September 1765, he recorded: 'Yesterday morning sent bold, spirited, noble letter to Porzia. At 10 1/2, Girolama. Alone: kind, concerted. You went away . . . Then Porzia at harpsichord. Was free. Got billets. Went out bold. Then Girolama. Quite agitated. Put on condom: entered. Heart beat; fell. Quite sorry, but said "A sign of true passion." Dined full to have courage; was feverish after it and did little all day.'

Probably because of this, Boswell had a higher opinion of Siena than most Grand Tourists. Horace Walpole dismissed the city in 1741 as 'bold, and very smug, with very few inhabitants'.

From *Italy: A Grand Tour for the Modern Traveller*,
CHARLES FITZROY

ROME

All the dreams of my youth I now behold realised before me.

GOETHE

Rome is beautiful, wonderful.

IBSEN

The senses are everywhere assailed; and the pavement, sprinkled with blood and filth, exhibits the entrails of pigs, or piles of stale fish, sold almost with the pale of the doorway.

LADY MORGAN

> *I wonder do you feel today*
> *As I have felt, since, hand in hand,*
> *We sat down on the grass, to stray*
> *In spirit better through the land,*
> *This morn of Rome and May?*

ROBERT BROWNING

The inhabitants of the mountains between Rome, Lake Turano, Aquila, and Ascoli, represent fairly well, to my way of thinking, the moral condition of Italy in about the year 1400.

STENDHAL

The lady in ecstasy all night in the next compartment and her extraordinary love cries 'the soft cries of love's delight' and I have never heard anything so demonstrative, so physical. (The old world can still teach the new) and in Rome three hours before the train to Naples and we had hot chocolate and muffins and then chartered a hack and saw the forum and the fish-market and churches and fountains so that we almost missed the Express.

Rome. To Saint Peter's (ugly, a dreary interior, no mysteriousness and a dwarf woman dressed in black.) At the Vatican S.V.R.C. nervous and unappreciative, H.M.C. interested in everything no matter what it was, and C and I hand in hand marvelling at a marble, and there was the Vatican Library and Torquato Tasso's autograph and a manuscript page of his poetry (he rhymed *fecondo* with *giocondo*) and later to visit with C the graves of Keats and Shelley and we laid daffodils and violets on their graves and kissed in the sun and she is sun-lovely and there was the Temple of the Vestal Virgins (and inside me the Temple of the Sun) and there was the Fontana Trevi into which we threw the littlest gold coin but I don't really know whether I ever want to return to Rome.

To the station one hour ahead of time (at S.V.R.C.'s insistence) and the Seven of Hearts in the Station (good omen) and the Parigi Celere, and so goodbye many-fountained Rome, and

the last thing we saw was the big pyramid in the English cemetery. Goodbye Shelley. Goodbye John Keats.

Mild sunny afternoon along the shore of the sea and
Livorno and Pisa at six o'clock with a glimpse of the Cathedral
and the leaning tower (like a soul that has been hurt by love)
and the tow-path that runs along the Arno towards Florence.
And there was a rose-brown, red-golden sunset and reflections
in the water, and Genoa and Turin and after innumerable tunnels (are there tunnels through the mountains of the heart?)
Modane.

From *Shadows of the Sun*, HARRY CROSBY

After leaving Florence I compared the solitude of Pisa with the
industry of Lucca and Leghorn, and continued my journey
through Sienna to Rome, where I arrived at the beginning of
October. My temper is not very susceptible to enthusiasm,
and the enthusiasm which I do not feel I have ever scorned to
affect. But, at the distance of twenty-five years, I can neither
forget nor express the strong emotions which agitated my mind
as I first approached and entered the *Eternal City*. After a sleep-
less night, I trod with a lofty step, the ruins of the Forum; each
memorable spot where Romulus stood, or Tully spoke, or
Caesar fell, was at once present to my eye; and several days of
intoxication were lost or enjoyed before I could descend to a
cool and minute investigation . . . It was at Rome, on the 15th
of October, 1764, as I sat musing amidst the ruins of the
Capitol while the barefooted friars were singing Vespers in the
Temple of Jupiter, that the idea of writing the decline and fall
of the city first started in my mind. But my original plan was

circumscribed to the decay of the city rather than that of the empire: and, though my reading and reflections began to point towards that object, some years elapsed and several avocations intervened, before I was seriously engaged in the execution of that laborious work.

EDWARD GIBBON

I had no idea that an excitement so powerful and agreeable still untried by me was to be found in the world.

MACAULAY

Rome was all dripping. Especially around the Tiber, from Testaccio to Porta Portese, to the Lungaretta. Rain fell, so dense and so fine that it dissolved before it hit the pavement. The avenues and the narrow side-streets were full of that hot steam, with the Aventine floating on one side and Monteverde on the other.

It was six or seven in the evening, so when Tommaso, Lello and Shitter got off the number 13 at the little garden opposite Ponte Quattro Capi, the place was deserted, or almost; there were only the first whores beginning to stroll around and some motorbikes cruising from Ponte Garibaldi to Caracalla. But once the boys had crossed the bridge, to the Lungaretta, there was all the usual Sunday-night confusion. The kids went by in bunches, coming out of the Cinema Reale, the Esperia, the Fontana, or from some of the cheap parish movies run by the priests, wandering around for a breath of air before going home to supper.

From *Una Vita Violenta*, PIER PAOLO PASOLINI

I met Smelfungus in the grand portico of the Pantheon – he was just coming out of it – "'tis nothing but a huge cock-pit', said he –

From *A Sentimental Journey*, LAURENCE STERNE

Then another time we went to Rome and we brought back a beautiful black renaissance plate. Maddalena, the old Italian cook, came up to Gertrude Stein's bedroom one morning to bring the water for her bath. Gertrude Stein had the hiccoughs. But cannot the signora stop it, Maddalena said anxiously. No, said Gertrude Stein between hiccoughs. Maddalena, shaking her head sadly, went away. In a minute there was an awful crash. Up flew Maddalena, oh signora, signora, she said, I was so upset because the signora had the hiccoughs that I broke the black plate that the signora so carefully brought from Rome. Gertrude Stein began to swear, she has a reprehensible habit of swearing whenever anything unexpected happens and she always tells me she learned it in her youth in California. She swore and the hiccoughs ceased. Maddalena's face was wreathed in smiles.

From *The Autobiography of Alice B. Toklas*, GERTRUDE STEIN

And now he has entered Rome, the sovereign of the world. The serpent rises erect, and lifts his neck that reclines against the top of the mast, and looks around for a habitation suited for himself. *There is a spot, where* the river flowing around, is divided into two parts; it is called 'The Island'. *The river*, in the direction of each side extends its arms of equal length, the dry land *lying* in the middle. Hither the serpent, son of Phoebus, betakes himself from the Laotian ship; and he puts an end to the mourning, having resumed his celestial form. And *thus* did he come, the restorer of health, to the City.

The Metamorphoses, OVID

Rome is the most glorious place in the universal world.

ROBERT ADAM

After lunch, return to the Piazza di Spagna and, if you have sufficient energy, climb the steep stairs to the Keats-Shelley Memorial Museum where Keats lived during the last months of his life. Reminders of Keats's tragic early death, his death-mask, and the manuscript of his poem 'Bright Star, were I as stedfast as thou art', bring his last months, spent wasting away in this apartment, vividly to life.

CHARLES FITZROY

With S. to the Villa Medici – perhaps on the whole the most enchanting place in Rome. The part of the garden called the Boschetto has an incredible, impossible charm; an upper terrace, behind locked gates, covered with a little dusky forest of evergreen oaks. Such a dim light as of a fabled, haunted place, such a soft suffusion of tender grey-green tones, such a company of gnarled and twisted little miniature trunks – dwarfs playing with each other at being giants – and such a shower of golden sparkles drifting in from the vivid West! At the end of the wood is a steep, circular mound, up which the short trees scramble amain, with a long mossy staircase climbing up to a belvedere.

. . . The blessing in Rome is not that this or that or the other isolated object is so very unsurpassable; but that the general air so contributes to interest, to impressions that are not as any other impressions anywhere in the world. And from this general air the Villa Medici has distilled an essence of its own – walled it in and made it delightfully private.

HENRY JAMES

Rome has vanquished me. By temperament as well as by instinct I have a need for the superfluous. My spiritual education draws me irresistibly to the desire for and the acquisition of beautiful things. I could quite easily have lived in a modest house, sat on Vienna chairs, eaten from ordinary plates, walked on carpets made in Italy, drunk tea from a threepenny cup. Instead and fatally, I have wanted divans, precious fabrics, Persian carpets, Japanese china, bronzes, ivories, knickknacks, all those useless and beautiful things which I love so deeply and passionately. I have done what I could not do. Rome has beaten me. I shall go back home.

GABRIELE D'ANNUNZIO

In the solitude of the Via Sacra the well-known objects seemed alien and ghost-like. But when I approached the grand ruins of the Colosseum and looked through the gate into the interior, I must frankly confess that a shudder ran through me, and I quickly returned home.

Any gigantic mass has a peculiar effect on me; it has something about it which is at once fascinating and awe-inspiring. I drew up a *summa summarum* of my whole stay in Italy, and this roused in my agitated soul a mood I might call heroic-elegiac, for it tried to embody itself in the poetic form of an elegy.

From *Italian Journey*, GOETHE

Italy was mostly an emotion and the emotion naturally centred in Rome. Rome, before 1870, was seductive beyond resistance. The month of May 1860 was divine . . . The shadows breathed and glowed, full of soft forms felt by lost senses.

HENRY JAMES

NAPLES

A little bit of heaven fallen upon the earth.

NEAPOLITAN SAYING

Then we came to the top of a ridge and a grand panorama unfolded before us: Naples in all its glory, rows of houses for miles along the flat coastline of the Gulf, promontories, headlands, cliffs, then the islands and, beyond them, the sea. A breath-taking sight!

Naples is a paradise; everyone lives in a state of intoxicated self-forgetfulness, myself included. I seem to be a completely different person whom I hardly recognise.

From *Italian Journey*, GOETHE

A country of fiddlers and poets, whores and scoundrels.

LORD HORATIO NELSON

Vesuvius windswept and full of fog. Down a rocky declivity and we could see the erupting volcano vomiting red blocks of lava which rattled and smouldered at our feet. The sound was the sound of a big shell bursting, the reverberation of thunder, the clanging of an iron door, and I was reminded of the war. Sulphur steam rose everywhere, heavy clouds poured downwards and hot lava sizzled and grew cold. We waited for four or five of these tremendous explosions which occurred about a minute apart then a terrific climb back up the precipitous path, exhausting in the high altitude. We reached the rack and pinion in time to catch the last train down and we were the only two who came up in our car who did what we did (the others could not have possibly seen anything due to the fog). Suicide in the actual crater of Vesuvius would be impossible (unless there was absolutely no erupting going on) as one would in nine cases out of ten be maimed before reaching the rim.

In a little station on the main line from Pompeii to Naples we saw a poor boy with a wooden leg who asked if he might shine our shoes and I gave him five lire and some crackers and now I wish I had given him more. Le Favori.

From *Shadows of the Sun*, HARRY CROSBY

Neapolitan painting was inspired by the arrival of Caravaggio in 1606, escaping the authorities in Rome, who wanted him on a charge of manslaughter. Two of his leading followers, Stanzione and Ribera, competed for the honour of painting a Pietà for the church. So excellent was their work that both paintings were accepted, Stanzione's hanging above the main door and Ribera's in the Treasury to the left of the choir. The rooms off the choir are in contrasting styles, some filled with intarsia work, others covered in brilliantly coloured frescos by Luca Giordano, known as 'Fa Presto' from the speed at which he worked.

CHARLES FITZROY

A paradise inhabited by devils.

JOSEPH FORSYTH

In 1558, a Venetian report lists in the Kingdom of Naples 24 dukes, 25 marquises, 90 counts, about 800 barons and of these, 13 noblemen had incomes of between 16,000 and 45,000 crowns. These figures later rose. In 1580 there were 11 princes, 25 dukes, 37 marquises; in 1597, 213 'titolati', consisting of 25 princes, 41 dukes, 75 marquises, 72 counts and 600 or more barons. Later one loses count altogether of this small fry.

San Gennaro, the patron saint of Naples, was martyred by Romans at Pozzuli during the pre-Christian era. Richard Gambino, a first-generation American who attended the *festa* of San Gennaro as a child, still recalls his fascination with the festivals: 'Their aromas of food, the sight of burly men swaying from side to side and lurching forward under the weight of enormous statues of exotic Madonnas and saints laden with money and gifts, the music of the Italian bands in uniforms with dark-peaked caps, white shirts, and black ties and the bright arches of colored lights spanning the city streets are essential memories of my childhood, as they are of many second-generation Italian Americans.'

From *La Storia: Five Centuries of the Italian American Experience*,

JERRE MANGIONE & BEN MORREALE

I was extremely delighted with the Museum of the things taken out of Herculaneum, but could steal nothing for you.

EARL OF CARLISLE

After dinner the king bows and retires and immediately drives away to a Palace near the town where he shoots every sparrow he can find.

WILLIAM BLACKETT

Naples is extraordinary in every way. At the end of the last century, Scarfoglio, leading Italian journalist of his day, wrote, 'This is the only Eastern city where there is no residential European quarter,' and the witticism still seems to hold good.

Last week a nobleman in our street was lifted by his servants from his deathbed, dressed in his evening clothes, then carried to be propped up at the head of the staircase over the courtyard of his palazzo. Here, with a bouquet of roses thrust into his arms, he stood for a moment to take leave of his friends and neighbours gathered in the courtyard below, before being carried back to receive the last rites. Where else but in Naples could a sense of occasion be carried to such lengths?

Last week, too, Evans and I were sent rummaging through the apartment of Prince Pignatelli. A satchel on a bedside table with a porphyry top contained half a million lire, and beside it stood a glass of wine into which gold leaf had been stirred. A cupboard held great flagons of Chanel perfume, and several hundred pairs of silk stockings, each pair worth the price of the honour of any woman in Naples whose honour was for sale. The impression this place gave was of the worship of luxury as a cult. A number of Neapolitan aristocrats claim descent from the great families of ancient Rome, and they may be still under the influence of legendary Roman excesses.

NORMAN LEWIS

Soon after his arrival at Naples, Sir Walter Scott went with his physician and one or two friends to the great museum. It happened that on the same day a large collection of students and Italian literati were assembled in one of the rooms to discuss some newly discovered manuscripts. It was soon known that the 'Wizard of the North' was there, and a deputation was sent immediately to request him to honour them by presiding at their session. At this time Scott was a wreck, with a memory that retained nothing for a moment, and limbs almost as helpless as an infant's. He was dragging about among the relics of Pompeii, taking no interest in any thing he saw, when the request was made known to him through his physician. 'No, no,' said he, 'I know nothing of their lingo. Tell them I am not well enough to come.' He loitered on, and in about half an hour he turned to Dr. H. and said, 'Who was that you said wanted to see me?' The doctor explained. 'I'll go,' said he, 'they shall see me if they wish it;' and against the advice of his friends, who feared it would be too much for his strength, he mounted the staircase, and made his appearance at the door. A burst of

enthusiastic cheers welcomed him on the threshold, and form-
ing two lines, many of them on their knees, they seized his
hands as he passed, kissed them, thanked him in their passionate language for the delight with which he had filled the world,
and placed him in the chair with the most fervent expressions of
gratitude for his condescension. The discussion went on; but
not understanding a syllable of the language Scott was soon
wearied and his friends, observing it, pleaded the state of his
health as an apology and he rose to take his leave. These enthusiastic children of the south crowded once more around him,
and with exclamations of affection and even tears kissed his
hands once more, assisted his tottering steps, and sent after
him a confused murmur of blessings as the door closed on his
retiring form. It is described by the writer as the most affecting
scene he had ever witnessed.

From an account of Sir Walter Scott's visit to Naples
by SIR WILLIAM GELL

Naples is set in the Campagna Felice, some of the most beautiful countryside in Europe, rich in classical associations and full
of interesting phenomena. For the eighteenth-century tourist
weaned on the classics, the combination proved irresistible. He
could visualise the landscape through the eyes of Virgil, who
had composed his *Georgics* and *Aeneid* in Naples, and imagine
the excesses of the Roman emperors, particularly Tiberius with
his boys on Capri and Caligula building a bridge of boats across
the Bay of Naples.

CHARLES FITZROY

EMILIA-ROMAGNA

Here all the cities are capitols, and have not that provincial tone of the secondary towns of other kingdoms.

BYRON

BOLOGNA

That celebrated mart of lapdogs and sausages.

WILLIAM BECKFORD

RAVENNA

Ravenna itself preserves more of the old Italian manners than any city in Italy – it is more out of the way of travellers and armies – and thus they have retained more of their originality. They make love a great deal – and assassinate a little.

BYRON

A miserable place, the people are barbarous and wild, and their language the most infernal patois that you can imagine.

SHELLEY

From the Mausoleum take the Via Carlo Cattaneo down the Via Cavour, turn left to reach the rather grim Palazzo Guiccioli

33

at no. 54, where Byron settled in 1820, paying Count Guiccioli a substantial rent for the privilege of making love to his wife. Perhaps he recalled his initial observation on his arrival in Italy, that 'a woman is virtuous (according to the code) who limits herself to her husband and one lover.'

Shelley came to visit Byron in August 1821 and recorded the extraordinary set-up in the palace.

CHARLES FITZROY

Lord B.'s establishment consists, besides servants, of ten horses, eight enormous dogs, three monkeys, five cats, an eagle, a crow, and a falcon, and all these, except the horses, walk about the house, which every now and then resounds with their unarbitrated quarrels, as if they were masters of it . . .

After I have sealed my letter, I find that my enumeration of the animals in this Circean Palace was defective, and that in a material point. I have just met on the grand staircase five peacocks, two guinea hens, and an Egyptian crane.

SHELLEY

VENICE

As night approached, innumerable tapers glimmered through the awnings before the windows. Every boat had its lantern, and the gondolas moving rapidly along were followed by tracks of light, which gleamed and played upon the waters. I was gazing at these dancing fires when the sounds of music were wafted

34

along the canals, and as they grew louder and louder, an illuminated barge, filled with musicians, issued from the Rialto, and stopping under one of the palaces, began a serenade, which stilled every clamour and suspended all conversation in the galleries and porticoes; till, rowing slowly away, it was heard no more. The gondoliers, catching the air, imitated its cadences, and were answered by others at a distance, whose voices, echoed by the arch of the bridge, acquired a plaintive and interesting tone. I retired to rest, full of the sound, and long after I was asleep, the melody seemed to vibrate in my ear.

WILLIAM BECKFORD

This miraculous city, lying in the bosom of the sea.

JOHN EVELYN

Grand Tourists were less than ecstatic about St Mark's, which they felt to be in bad taste. Président de Brosses, typical of his age's preference for order and harmonious proportions, criticised it for being 'in the Greek style, low, impenetrable to the light, in wretched taste both within and without', and compared the cupolas to copper kettles. In 1802, Eustace took a more romantic view of the interior, praising 'its gloomy, barbaric magnificence'.

CHARLES FITZROY

A grand and dreamy structure; redolent of perfumes; dim with the smoke of incense; costly in treasure of precious stones and metals, glittering through iron bars; holy with the bodies of deceased saints; rainbow-hued with windows of stained glass;

dark with carved woods and coloured marbles; obscure in its vast heights and lengthened distances, shining with silver lamps and winking lights; unreal, fantastic, solemn, inconceivable thought.

CHARLES DICKENS

A veritable Golden Book on whose monumental facade the entire Venetian nobility has signed its name.

THÉOPHILE GAUTIER

A low and monotonous dockyard wall, with flat arches to let the tide through it.

RUSKIN (on the railway bridge across the lagoon)

My tendency to look at the world through the eyes of the painter whose pictures I have seen last has given me an odd idea. Since our eyes are educated from childhood on by the objects we see around us, a Venetian painter is bound to see the world as a brighter and gayer place than most people see it. We northerners who spend our lives in a drab and, because of the dirt and dust, an uglier country where even reflected light is subdued, and who have, most of us, to live in cramped rooms – we cannot instinctively develop an eye which looks with such delight at the world.

GOETHE

Of all the spectacular food markets in Italy the one near the Rialto in Venice must be the most remarkable. The light of a Venetian dawn in early summer – you must be about at four o'clock in the morning to see the market coming to life – is so limpid and so still that it makes every separate vegetable and fruit and fish luminous with a life of its own, with unnaturally heightened colours and clear stencilled outlines. Here the cabbages are cobalt blue, the beetroots deep rose, the lettuces clear pure green, sharp as glass. Bunches of gaudy gold marrowflowers, green plums, green peas. The colours of the peaches, cherries and apricots, packed in boxes lined with sugar-bag blue paper matching the blue canvas trousers worn by the men unloading the gondolas, are reflected in the rose-red mullet and the orange *vongole* and *canestrelle* which have been prised out of their shells and heaped into baskets.

From *Italian Food*, ELIZABETH DAVID

Travelled through sewers in a coffin.

OSCAR WILDE

SICILY

An uninterrupted succession of desperate impulses and supine submissions, of rapid, brightly-lit moments and zones interminably dark.

SEBASTIANO AGLIANÒ (on Sicilian history)

As in certain sweet and savoury dishes that contain everything, where the savoury merges into the sweet and the sweet into the savoury, dishes that seem to realize a hungry man's dream, so the most abundant and overflowing markets, the richest and most festive and the most baroque, are those of the poor countries where the spectre of hunger is always hovering . . . in Baghdad, Valencia or Palermo, a market is more than a market . . . it's a vision, a dream, a mirage.

The market the Sicilian writer Leonardo Sciascia had in mind here was the Vucciria. It'd been like a dream when I first wandered into it at the end of an earlier summer years and years ago. Whenever I went back to Palermo, the market was the first place I headed for. It was a way of getting my bearings. The first time, twenty-one years earlier, I'd arrived in Palermo mapless from Enna, in the high, parched, bleak centre of the island, the poorest province in Italy, and strayed through the ruins of the old city. The old city of Palermo had been gutted by bombs in 1943, in the months before the allied armies invaded Sicily. A lot of its finest buildings, palazzi of the seventeenth and eighteenth centuries, the family homes of the Sicilian nobility, about a third of them were destroyed.

Other European cities had been bombed in the forties, and many worse than Palermo. What was unique in Palermo was that the ruins of the old city were still ruins, thirty years, fifty years on. Staircases still led nowhere, sky shone out of the windows, clumps of weed lodged in the walls, wooden roof beams jutted towards the sky like the ribs of rotting carcasses. Slowly, even the parts that had survived were crumbling into the rubble. There were more people living there in the early seventies in the buildings that were still intact, or partly so, and it must've been a Monday because the washing was strung across the alleys like flags, whipping and billowing everywhere in the powerful sun. It was a very hot day when I stepped into the Vucciria from a narrow crooked alley, it was a move from the wings onto a stage set in mid-show.

PETER ROBB

The *Vucciria* is a painting I'd been carrying around inside me for years. I come from Bagheria, but I went to a high school in Palermo. In the morning I used to go to the market for my lunch, I bought bread and *panelle*. The market stalls fascinated me, their displays of Sicilian fruit and vegetables. I thought of doing a canvas like a great still life, with a path cut through it like a groove and people buying and looking. The idea took over, and there's too much still life in the picture. Too many peppers, too many tomatoes, too many eggs.

RENATO GUTTOSO

> *In your homeland, Guttoso, the moon has the smell*
> *of white grapes, honey and fallen lemons*
> *but there is no land*
> *there is no bread.*

PABLO NERUDA

The pearl of the century for abundance and beauty, the first country in the world for its nature, its buildings and its antiquity. Travellers come from everywhere, merchants and dealers from every city and metropolis, and all agree in praising it, and praise its splendid beauty, speak of its happy circumstances, its various advantages and the good things Sicily attracts from every other country in the world.

39

The huge and beautiful city, the greatest and most splendid place to stay, the vastest and finest city in the world . . . It lies on the sea in the western part of the island. High mountains surround it, and yet its shore is joyous, sunny, smiling. Palermo has such beautiful buildings that travellers come to admire the architecture, the exquisite workmanship, the art . . . All around the city are streams and perpetual springs. Inside the town are many gardens, beautiful houses and canals of fresh running water, brought from the mountains that surround its plain. Outside the southern side runs the ever-flowing Abbas (Oreto) river, which has enough mills built along it to fully satisfy all the city's needs.

ABU ABDULLAH MUHAMMAD IBN IDRIS

You used to hear the cry, *Snow from Cammarata, snow from Cammarata* as soon as the June heat became suffocating. Cammarata is a mountain town, very high up, and the snow that was gathered there arrived in Racalmuto on carts between two layers of salt and straw. Salt and straw were used to insulate and preserve the snow. And at home too it was covered in straw to make it last longer. It was used to cool the wine and make granitas. A handful of snow was splashed with blackcurrant or gooseberry syrup, that kids particularly loved. You used to hold it in the hollow of your hand and swallow it quickly before it melted. At home there were even special bottles with an inside compartment you put the snow in, so you could drink cool wine at the height of summer. When the ice factory was built in the thirties, the kids missed the snow from Cammarata but they loved . . . the blocks of ice sliding along the conveyer belt. And for a penny they gave you a bit of grated ice with syrup.

LEONARDO SCIASCIA

With S.V.R.C. to the Catacombs (escorted by a monk) and the skeletons were entirely dressed and whiskers and beards and eyebrows were often apparent and virgins wore tin crowns on their heads and there were babies and there were priests in red velvet and it was weird.

With H.M.C. to the Marionettes in a toy theatre, a room the size of the cock-fight room in Seville, a room divided into stage, pit and gallery (where we sat). The audience (about 150) composed of men and boys, H.M.C. being the only woman in the house unless we count the old hag who sold tickets (one lira each) at the entrance. Everyone wore caps and nearly everyone smoked. The pit was crowded and people sat on rude benches. Cobwebs hung from the faded blue ceiling (*ciel de lit*). The walls were white-washed. A mechanical hurdy-gurdy rendered dreary music and everyone talked. As the footlights went out the tawdry curtains (representing the Rape of the Sabine Women) went up. A final crash from the hurdy-gurdy, then it ceased and a marionette appeared, a young knight clad in silver armour. He appeared to be trying to rescue a lady (also in armour) who was bound in chains and who was about to be decapitated. And there ensued a hand to hand fight between the knight and the executioners and there was much clashing of sabres and slicing off of heads and there were rival knights and more crossing of swords and at the end the young knight carried off the fair captive and it was all

41

very quaint and primitive – the set faces of the marionettes, their strange gestures, the glimpses of the huge hands of the manipulators, the various tones of the ventriloquist's voice, the classic simplicity of the subject, and the breathlessness of the audience.

Girgenti. Never never never never want to see Palermo again. Here the Temple of Juno and the Temple of Concord and inside me the Temple of the Sun.

Syracuse. The Roman Amphitheatre, the Ear of Dionysius and the Greek theatre, the Amphitheatre for cruelty, the cavern-prison for ingenuity, the Greek theatre for thought, and here it was that Pindar sang his odes, here it was the multitude watched the great battle in the harbor, and here it was that Timoleon of Corinth gave counsel to the people. The Ear of Dionysius suggests a sonnet, the octave to show how the tyrant listened to the whispering of his prisoners, the sextet to compare a beautiful lady to him, listening to the prisoners of her heart. Think of this cavern dating from 400 B.C.!

A tempest is raging in the Ionian Sea and I was disappointed in the Venus Anadyomene and I snatched a jawbone from a skeleton lying in an open sarcophagus (this for my dentist for the teeth seemed in good condition), and later on with H.M.C. in a painted boat up the Cyane where the papyrus grow in abundance, and before supper a walk in the ancient quarries and they reminded me of the Arabian Nights and there were orange trees (The Orange Tree hath in her sightly fruit The colours Daphne boasted in her hair).

Taormina and all Sicilian disillusions vanish and the shops

are fascinating and the peasants are quaint, the streets and houses picturesque, and all the countryside is pink with almond blossoms.

From *Shadows of the Sun*, HARRY CROSBY

Bronze archangels looking over my shoulder, I sat one muggy day in Palermo on the cool white steps at the base of piazza San Domenico's monument to the Virgin and worried at Sciascia's words about the painting of *La Vucciria*, or rather the Vucciria market itself, the hungry man's dream just out of sight below me. Sciascia had mentioned 'certain sweet and savour dishes that contain everything, where the savoury merges into the sweet and the sweet into the savour.' With their suggestion of gorgeous fantasy anchored in a palpably sensuous reality, something out of the *Arabian Nights*, the words were wildly romantic and at the same time domestic, familiar. What was Sciascia talking about? Then I remembered *caponata*.

The caponata I first knew had been a cheap cold dish eaten at night at a trestle table amid the traffic at Porta Cappuana in Naples, a change from steamed muscles. Anchovy and chopped octopus tentacles and black Gaeta olives, with a bit of salad and some broth slopped over a flat and rocklike hard biscuit. Elizabeth David describes this accurately as 'primitive fisher-man's and sailor's dishes.' She called it *caponata all marinara*. It was only when craning over a neighbouring table once, under the fluorescent lights of the Horse Shoe, through the flying bread and the slamming plates and the wine-splashed paper cloths, that I realized caponata in Palermo was something very different. It was the colour that struck me first. The colour of darkness. A heap of cubes of that unmistakable luminescent dark, dark purply-reddish goldy richness, glimmerings from a baroque canvas, that comes from eggplant, black olives, tomato and olive oil densely cooked together, long and gently. The colour of southern Italian cooking. Caponata was one of the world's great sweet and sour dishes, sweet, sour and savour.

The eggplant was the heart of caponata. The celery hearts were the most striking component: essential and surprising. Pieces of each were fried separately in olive oil until they were a fine golden colour and then added to a sauce made by cooking tomato, sugar and vinegar with a golden chopped onion in oil and adding Sicilian olives, capers and *bottarga*, which was tuna roe dried into a block and sliced or shaved or grated for use. This, however, was only the beginning of the full caponata. I doubted whether any prized bottarga was grated into the one the Horse Shoe served up daily in great quantities for next to nothing. The Horse Shoe's was delicious, but essentially a vegetable dish. I used to eat it with their boiled beef. Elizabeth David had a perfunctory version from a French cook book of 1913, which got it from the German ambassador's cook in Rome. She presented it with a very interesting English putdown: 'An interesting dish . . . Try it in half quantities.'

A Palermitan wrote that 'he who has not eaten a caponata of eggplant has never reached the antechamber of the terrestrial paradise.' He described its taste as ' . . . a composite flavour comparable to no other, but which recalls nostalgically exotic lands and seas, whose mingled aromas evoke the chief characteristic of Sicilian cuisine, the field on which all the other cuisines give battle to each other.'

PETER ROBB

To have seen Italy without having seen Sicily is not to have seen Italy at all, for Sicily is the clue to everything.

GOETHE

. . . your only mistake was saying 'the Sicilians must want to improve' . . . the Sicilians never want to improve for the simple reason that they think themselves perfect; their vanity is stronger than their misery . . .

From *The Leopard*, GIUSEPPE DI LAMPEDUSA

At no point on earth, I'm sure, has sky ever stretched more violently blue than it did above our enclosed terrace, never has sun thrown gentler rays than those penetrating the half-closed shutters of the 'green drawing-room', never have damp-marks on a courtyard's outer walls presented shapes more stimulating to the imagination than those at my home.

I loved everything about it: the irregularity of its walls, the number of its drawing-rooms, the stucco of its ceilings, the nasty smell from my grandparents' kitchen, the scent of violets in my mother's dressing-room, the stuffiness of its stables, the good feel of polished leather in its tack-rooms, the mystery of some unfinished apartments on the top floor, the huge coach-house in which our carriages were kept; a whole world full of sweet mysteries, of surprises ever renewed and ever fresh.

I was its absolute master and would run continually through its vast expanses, climbing the great staircase from the courtyard to the loggia on the roof, from which could be seen the sea and Mount Pellegrino and the whole city as far as Porta Nuova and Monreale.

From *The Siren and selected writings*, LAMPEDUSA

American Superfortresses flew over Palermo on 5th April 1943. It was the bombing raid that destroyed a good third of the old city centre, a prelude to the coming invasion. The palazzo Lampedusa received a direct hit and Lampedusa's material link to the world of childhood, family and the past was gone. After Lampedusa saw the ruins, he walked twenty kilometres to the Prince of Mirto's house by the sea near Bagheria, at Santa Flavia. Lampedusa arrived filthy with dust and unrecognizable, and according to Count Sarzana, who was there, sat three days without speaking a word. Although Lampedusa mourned its destruction for the rest of his life, the physical loss of his family palace, like the sale twenty years earlier of the palace at Santa Margherita di Belice, where he'd spent his childhood summers, were the necessary events that freed his imagination. The lost palace at Santa Margherita, sold to a hostile family to pay the debts of his socialist uncle, was transformed into the Donnafugata of the novel Lampedusa was to write. The death of his mother, the dominating dowager princess, in 1947, may have been equally liberating.

Without this violent loss, without this clearing of the ground, his imagination may never have been so deeply engaged.

The more sensuously the vanished past was evoked, the more implacably his intelligence resisted, heightening the tension in the language until the novel transformed itself into an examination of life and death in Sicily, one that closed in a mood of sublime and unSicilian levity. Lampedusa, like Proust, made sensuous recall the means to understanding and not to consolation. Like Proust, he had a formidable intellect. A group of student friends had been drawn to the pale and taciturn prince, who was described around this time as looking like a retired general. Realizing they 'knew nothing', as he put it, he'd also delved into his life's reading and written a series of lectures on English and French writers they read together in the evenings. The man who was old in his fifties, remembered by Bassani for 'the bitter twist to his lips,' opened out to these young people. One of them he adopted, perpetuating his titles, and made *The Leopard's* quick, ironic and ambitious Tancredi in his likeness.

Tancredi is the penniless young aristocrat who rises through his wit with a strategic marriage to the beautiful daughter of a newly-rich mafioso. He's the nephew of Don Fabrizio, the prince the novel revolves around, a tall, fair, idealized alter ego of its writer. The novel's action pivots on the historical moment of Garibaldi's unification of Italy. Nothing much happens in *The Leopard.* The big events are anticipated or looked back on or heard of from afar. Small domestic things refract an image of the big world outside. The prince's family move to their country estate for summer. They hold a dinner-party for the locals. The prince goes rabbit shooting. Tancredi and his fiancee Angelica wander through the deserted rooms of the palace.

Don Fabrizio turns down an invitation to join the Italian senate. There is a ball in Palermo.

'The burnished gold of the outside and the fragrance exuded of sugar and cinnamon were only preludes to the sensation of delight released from the interior when the knife slit the crust; aroma-charged steam burst out first, then chicken livers, little hard boiled eggs, fillets of ham, chickens and truffles could all be seen embedded in the mass of hot and glistening short macaroni, that the meat juice gave an exquisite soft brown tinge.'

From *Midnight in Sicily*, PETER ROBB

Lampedusa felt passionately that melodrama had destroyed the Italians' sensibility to art and made them impervious to the subtlety of fine writing. Jane Austen, for instance, was not appreciated in Italy because she was *l'antimelodramma*; Italians consequently complained that nothing happened in her novels. The problem so engrossed Lampedusa that one day he decided he had to write down his objections to melodrama in order to stop himself lying awake at night.

The infection began immediately after the Napoleonic wars and spread with giant steps. For more than a hundred years, tens of thousands, hundreds of thousands of Italians went to the opera, in the great cities for eight months a year and in the small towns for two or three weeks each year. And they saw tyrants killed, lovers committing suicide, generous clowns, multiparous nuns and every sort of nonsense dished out in front of them in a continual whirling of cardboard boots, plaster-cast chickens, leading ladies with blackened faces and devils springing from the ground making awful grimaces. All this synthesized, without psychological passages, into developments, all bare, crude and irrefutable.

This unfathomable stupidity was not considered as common enjoyment, as an excusable distraction for illiterate layabouts; it was passed off as Art, as real Art, and horrors! sometimes it really was Art. The cancer had absorbed all the artistic energies of the nation: Music was Opera, Drama was Opera, Painting was Opera. And other musical forms like the symphony and chamber music languished and died: during the nineteenth century Italy lacked all of them. The drama which, with its slow build-ups, could not resist the waves of *Do di petto,* also died. Painters neglected their noble canvases to throw themselves headlong into designing the prisons of *Don Carlos* or the sacred groves of *Norma.*

When Opera mania diminished after 1910, Italian intellectual life was like a field in which locusts had spent a hundred years in a row. Italians had become accustomed to citing as gospel truth the lines of Francesco Mario Piave or Cammarono; to thinking that Enrico Caruso or Adelina Patti were the flowers of the race; and to believing that War was like the chorus of *Norma.* The influence of all this on the national character is before our eyes.

Art had to be easy and the music singable. Drama consisted of sword-thrusts flavoured with musical trills. What was not simple, violent, within the grasp equally of a professor and a dustman, was beyond the pale.

But there was worse than this. Saturated and swollen-headed by so much noisy foolishness, the Italians sincerely believed that they knew everything. Did they not go almost every evening that God gave them to listen to Shakespeare, Schiller, Victor Hugo and Goethe? Signor Gattoni from Milan or Cavaliere Pantisi from Palermo were convinced that universal literature had been revealed to them because they knew the above-mentioned poets having heard them through the notes of Verdi and Gounod . . . And so now we are the nation least interested in literature that exists, fed up (or so it seems) with Opera, but unready to listen to anything else.

Lampedusa saw Sicily as the victim of its size and geographical position. Since early classical times, Sicily has been too small and weak to defend itself, and yet too large, too strategically important and (until the later Middle Ages) too fertile to escape the interest of foreign powers. Its destiny has thus inevitably been colonial. [He wrote] 'We are old, Chevalley, very old. For over twenty-five centuries we've been bearing the weight of superb and heterogeneous civilizations, all from outside, none made by ourselves, none that we could call our own. We're as white as you are, Chevalley, and as the Queen of England; and yet for two thousand five hundred years we've been a colony. I don't say that in complaint; it's our fault. But even so we're worn out and exhausted . . .'

The 'impermeability to anything new', which Lampedusa recognized as a traditional Sicilian trait, seemed to him a consequence of the island's numerous foreign conquests and the imposition of alien civilizations. There were too many monuments and too many invaders, seldom resisted and always misunderstood, which produced a sense of fatalism among Sicilians.

The Leopard's success was unprecedented in Italy: twenty years after its publication, it had sold over a million copies, had gone through 121 editions, and been translated twenty-three times. In a 'referendum' held by an Italian literary weekly in 1985, it was voted 'the most loved as well as one of the two most important' Italian novels of the twentieth century.

From *The Last Leopard*, DAVID GILMOUR

A SENTIMENTAL JOURNEY

There is not a secret so aiding to the progress of sociality, as to get master of this *short hand*, and be quick in rendering the several turns of looks and limbs, with all their inflections and delineations, into plain words. For my own part, by long habitude, I do it so mechanically, that when I walk the streets of London, I go translating all the way; and have more than once stood behind in the circle, where not three words have been said, and have brought off twenty different dialogues with me, which I could have fairly wrote down and sworn to.

I was going one evening to Martini's concert at Milan, and was just entering the door of the hall, when the Marquesina di F . . . was coming out in a sort of hurry – she was almost upon me before I saw her; so I gave a spring to one side to let her pass. She had done the same, and on the same side too; so we ran our heads together: she instantly got to the other side to get out: I was just as unfortunate as she had been; for I had sprung to that side, and opposed her passage again – we both flew together to the other side, and then back – and so on – it was ridiculous; we both blush'd intolerably; so I did at last the thing I should have done at first – I stood stock still, and the Marquesina had no more difficulty. I had no power to go into the room, till I had made her so much reparation as to wait and follow her with my eye to the end of the passage. She look'd back twice, and walk'd along it rather sideways, as if she would make room for anyone coming up stairs to pass her. No, said I – that's a vile translation: the Marquesina has a right to the best apology I can make her; and that opening is left for me to do it in – so I ran and begg'd pardon for the embarrassment I had given her, saying it was my intention to have made her way. She answered, she was guided by the same intention towards me – so we reciprocally thank'd each other. She was at the top of the stairs; and seeing no *chichesbeo* near her, I begg'd to hand her to her coach – so we went down the stairs, stopping every third step to talk of the concert and the adventure – Upon my word, Madame, said I when I had handed her in, I made six different efforts to let you get out – And I made six efforts, replied she, to let you enter – I wish to heaven you would make a seventh, said I – With all my heart, she said, making room – Life is too short to be long about the forms of it – so I instantly stepp'd in and she carried me home with her – And what became of the concert, St Cecilia, who, I suppose was at it, knows more than I.

I will only add, that the connection which arose out of that translation, gave me more pleasure than anyone I had the honour to make in Italy.

LAURENCE STERNE

ITALIAN FOOD

The origins of Italian cooking are Greek, Roman, and to a lesser extent, Byzantine and Oriental.

The Romans, having evolved their cookery from the sane traditions of Greece, proceeded in the course of time to indulge in those excesses of gluttony which are too well known to bear repetition here; but what in fact must have been a considerable understanding of the intricacies of cookery has been overlooked in the astonishment of less robust ages at their gigantic appetites and at the apparently grotesque dishes they consumed. Owing to the necessities of preservation, a good deal of the food of those days must have been intolerably salty; to counteract this, and also presumably to disguise a flavour which must often have been none too fresh, the Romans added honey, sweet wine, dried fruit, and vinegar to meat, game and fish, which were, besides, heavily spiced and perfumed with musk, amber, pepper, coriander, rue.

Similar methods of cookery prevailed in all the more primitive parts of Europe until the nineteenth century, when the development of rapid transport began to make the large-scale salting and pickling of food unnecessary. In Italy, Roman tastes are still echoed in the *agrodolce* or sweet-sour sauces which the Italians like with wild boar, hare and venison. The Roman taste for little song-birds – larks, thrushes and nightingales – also persists in Italy to this day; so does the cooking with wine, oil and cheese, and the Roman fondness for pork, veal, and all kinds of sausages . . .

The spice trade, which had originated with the Phoenicians and never entirely died out, had a lasting influence on Italian cookery . . .

The term 'Italian' used in relation to food would in fact mean very little to most Italians. To them there is Florentine cooking, Venetian cooking; there are the dishes of Genoa, Piedmont, Romagna; of Rome, Naples and the Abruzzi; of Sardinia and Sicily; of Lombardy, Umbria, and the Adriatic coast. United Italy was created only in 1861, and not only have the provinces retained their own traditions of cookery, but many of their products remain localized.

In London or Paris can be found (or *could* be, before the system of export and import became so fanciful) the best of everything which England or France produces. In Italy the best fish is actually to be eaten on the coast, the finest Parmesan cheese in and around Parma, the tenderest beef in Tuscany, where the cattle are raised. So the tourist, having arrived in Italy via Naples and there mistakenly ordered a beef steak which turns out to be a rather shrivelled slice of veal, will thereafter avoid *bistecca*, so that when he visits Florence he will miss that remarkable *bistecca alla Fiorentino*, a vast steak, grilled over a wood fire, which, tender and aromatic, is a dish worth going some way to eat. How many transatlantic travellers landing in Genoa have dined in some Grand Hotel or other and gone on their way without ever suspecting that Genoa possesses a cookery of a most highly individual nature, unique in Europe? Everyone has heard of the *mortadella* sausage of Bologna, but how many hurrying motorists drive past the rose and ochre coloured arcades of Bologna, quite unaware that behind modest doorways are some of the best restaurants in Italy? Alas for them, they will remain ignorant of those remarkable dishes consisting of a breast of chicken or turkey cooked in butter, smothered with fine slices of those white truffles which are one of the glories of Italian cooking. Every Italian restaurant abroad serves a dish of so called *tagliatelle Bolognese*; it is worth visiting Bologna to find out what this dish really tastes like, and to accompany it with a bottle of that odd but delicious Lambrusco wine which combines so well with the rich Bolognese cooking. In Venice, nursing aggrieved memories of woolly Mediterranean fish, the traveller will refuse sole on the grounds that it can be eaten only in London or Paris. He will miss a treat, for the soles of the Adriatic have a particularly fine flavour. In Parma he will scarcely fail to eat Parma ham; but if he is not sufficiently inquisitive he will not taste another first-class local speciality, the Felino *salame*, which is one of the most excellent sausages produced in Italy. Now, the blame for this state of affairs lies, to a certain extent with the waiters and restaurant keepers. So convinced are these gentlemen that foreigners will accept only spaghetti in tomato sauce, to be followed by a veal cutlet, that the traveller, unless of an unusually determined nature, gives in over and over again, and finally returns home with the conviction that there is nothing else to be had in the whole country.

In Italy, therefore, it is worth finding out what is to be had in the locality in the way of wines, cheeses, hams, sausages, fruit, and vegetables. They should be asked for, if possible, beforehand; but at the same time it must be borne in mind that, as in any country which relies largely on its own agricultural produce, the seasonal character of the food remains intact . . .

When about to embark on my travels, English friends who knew Italy far better than I did at the time had been ready with unencouraging predictions: 'All that *pasta*,' they said. 'We've got enough stodge here already; you won't find much else in Italy. You'll have to invent.'

How we cling to our myths, we English. The French, we believe, have been forced to perfect the art of cooking owing to what we like to think is a necessity to disguise poor materials. We ourselves have, we comfortably imagine, no need for either art or artifice in the kitchen. Our basic ingredients are too superb to need the application of intelligence or training to their preparation. As for the Italians, they live, according to our mythology, on veal and tomatoes, spaghetti, cheese and olive oil.

In the original edition of *Household Management*, published in 1861, the very year of the unification of Italy under the rule of the House of Savoy, young Mrs Beeton asserted that 'modern Romans are merged in the general name of Italians, who, with the exception of macaroni, have no specially characteristic article of food'. She was expressing, no doubt, the general belief of her day – and, I fancy, very largely of our own, one hundred years on . . .

The difficulties of reproducing Italian cooking abroad are much the same as the difficulties attendant upon any good cooking outside its country of origin, and usually they can be overcome.

Italians, unlike the thrifty French, are very extravagant with raw materials. Butter, cheese, oil, the best cuts of meat, chicken and turkey breasts, eggs, chicken and meat broth, raw and cooked ham are used not so much with reckless abandon as with a precise awareness of what good quality does for cooking.

In most Italian households the marketing is done twice a day. Everything is freshly cooked for every meal. What the Italian kitchen misses in the form of concentrated meat glazes, *fumets* of fish and game, the *fonds de cuisine* of the French, it makes up for in the extreme freshness and lavishness of its raw materials. It is worth bearing in mind that when an Italian has not the wherewithal to cook one of the traditional extravagant dishes, she doesn't attempt to produce an imitation. No amount of propaganda could persuade her to see the point of making, let us say, a steak and kidney pudding with tinned beef and no kidneys, neither would she bother to make a ravioli stuffing with leftovers because the results would not at all resemble the dish as it should be, and would therefore be valueless. So her method would be to produce some attractive and nourishing little dish out of two ounces of cheese and a slice of ham, or a pound of spinach and a couple of eggs . . .

In April 1911 that perspicacious English gourmet Colonel Newnham Davis wrote that 'an Italian gentleman never eats salad when travelling in foreign countries, for his palate, used to the finest oil, revolts against the liquid fit only for the lubrication of machinery he so often is offered in Germany, England, and France . . .'

The great galleys of Venice and Florence
Be well laden with things of complacence:
All spicerye and of grocers ware
With sweet wines, all manner of fare

ADAM DE MOLYNEAUX

Peel a fig for your friend, a peach for your enemy.

ITALIAN PROVERB

To eat figs off the tree in the very early morning, when they have been barely touched by the sun, is one of the exquisite pleasures of the Mediterranean.

There are wonderful figs to be found all over Italy. The figs of Sicily are celebrated. There is a certain garden in Anacapri where the fig trees bear round purple figs which are not much to look at; their skins are mapped with fine lines, but the fruit cracks gently as it is picked, disclosing rose madder flesh which is sweet with a dry aftertaste, and these are the most lovely of all figs to eat with Parma ham . . .

The origins of Grana, or Parmesan, cheese must be very remote. The Parmesans claim that it has been made in the district for two thousand years. In any case it was already well known in the fourteenth century, when one of Boccaccio's characters, mocking the ignorance of one Calendrino, tells him that at Bengodi (in the province of Parma) 'there is a mountain consisting entirely of grated Parmesan cheese . . . on which live people who do nothing but make maccheroni and ravioli, and cook it in capon broth.'

The fame of Parma cheese as a condiment for *pasta* and rice and all cooked dishes is due to the fact that it does not form elastic threads as it melts, an almost unique property amongst cheeses; it will keep for years, and the older it is the better . . .

As for Naples, the city we know today as a place of decayed palaces and ugly slums where no car, however securely locked, is safe from theft, and where every foreigner is the target of ceaseless and aggressive begging, in the seventeenth century and right up to the end of the eighteenth and the days when Sir William Hamilton married his Emma and young Admiral Nelson appeared on the scene, nearly every visitor who set eyes on the place pronounced it the finest capital of all the Italian states . . .

Neapolitans lived well, importing any delicacies they couldn't produce within their own territories. 'The custom of hearbes spent yearly in Naples amounteth to foure thousand pounds of our money' reported the English traveller George Sandys in his *Relation of a Journey* published in 1611, and according to the French historian Fernand Braudel, in the year 1625 alone Naples imported 1,500 tons of sugar and 500 tons of honey . . .

Another import, and one which may have gone some way to account for the high consumption of sugar, was the chocolate so much loved by the Spaniards. Coming relatively early to Naples, and well established there by the last decade of the seventeenth century it was served sometimes hot, sometimes cold, even at the receptions held out of doors on warm evenings in those famous scented seaside gardens . . .

In 1694 Latini commented that 'in the city of Naples, a great quantity of sorbette is consumed, they are the consistency of sugar and snow, and every Neapolitan, it would appear, is born knowing how they are made.'

In Latini's world of Spanish administrators, Neapolitan noblemen and their families, government officials and high-ranking naval officers, ices were invariably prepared for early evening collations, very often alfresco ones served in the grounds of great seaside palaces, and made in quantity. In the shade of lemon and orange groves, among the scented roses for which the gardens of Naples were then famous, the richly-dressed ladies and gentlemen and their children would stroll and talk and play, the sea shimmering below in the evening sunlight, the islands of Ischia and Capri scarcely visible in the hazy distance, in the foreground the plume of smoke rising from Vesuvius to remind them of the ever-present menace of the volcano . . .

I suppose not every foreigner who visited Rome, Venice, Florence and Naples during the five centuries when Italy was first on the list of places to be seen kept a journal and later published it, but looking along the packed stacks of travel and topographical books devoted in any great library to Italy, or merely studying the subject index, one does get the impression that most of them did.

In May 1770, Patrick Brydone wrote to Beckford about a flowering shrub growing in great plenty around Messina. 'The fruit of this plant is beautiful, round, and of a bright shining yellow. They call it *pomo d'oro* or golden apple . . .'

'What enchanting names they have, these wines of Italy that roll off the tongue like poetry: Lacrima Christi, Albana, Capri, Montepulciano, San Gimignano. Not always so beautiful to taste, but some distinctly good, and a few fine.'

Those carefully chosen words are quoted from a book of light-hearted gastronomic reminiscences entitled *Food and other Frailties* by Romilly Fedden, an English painter who died in the early 1940s . . .

Addison found the wine of the Republic of San Marino extraordinarily good and 'much better than any I met with on the cold side of the Appenines' . . .

One white wine of Tuscany which is a curiosity, although one which has been known in the region since Dante's day, is the Vernaccia of San Gimignano. The vernaccia grape, cultivated on the hillsides around San Gimignano, makes deep straw-coloured wine with a flavour which has always seemed to me rather odd, and a taste for it is one which I have never quite acquired. At one time I went often to San Gimignano, where the hotel waiters expect you to drink Vernaccia all through every meal. Personally, I find that a little goes a long way and no amount of reflection that this was the wine that Chaucer knew as *vernage*, and that Dante too was familiar with it, could quite convince me that it goes well with modern Italian food. But you cannot go to San Gimignano of the Beautiful Towers and not try its very own and famous wine . . .

The wonderful fruits of Italy particularly impressed Hester Piozzi. Writing in the summer of 1785, when she was in Florence, she marvelled at the size of the cherries, as large as plums, and in a street market sees somebody's manservant 'weighing two in a scale to see if they came to an ounce'. The figs too were perfection, not by superior size, for they were small and green, but in taste and colour, 'a bright full crimson within, and we eat them with raw ham. I mean ham cured, not boiled or roasted'. Everywhere the bounty of Italian provisions, fruit and vegetables in particular, strikes Mrs Piozzi. 'Vegetable nature flourishes in full perfection, while every step crushes out perfume from the trodden herbs . . . The scent of truffles attracts, and the odour of melons gratifies one's nerves when driving among the habitations of fertile Lombardy. . .'

It was the autumn of 1963. With my old friend Viola Johnson I had been on a brief visit to Alba to eat the famous white truffles, and now we were due to return to London. In those days there were direct flights between London and Turin, and that circumstance provided a good opportunity for Viola to see her father who still lived in his native city, where she had herself been born and brought up. But at this moment we were shopping for small gifts to take home to England.

Strolling down the Via Roma, where the confectioners' shops were at the time famous, we stopped to admire a particularly tempting display of fondants, pink and white, coffee and lemon and lilac-coloured, and alluring chocolate made in imitation of chestnuts, truffles and hazelnuts. (Turin is the home of the delectable *gianduia*, those celebrated chocolates filled with a soft, melting, rich and buttery hazelnut paste.) Also in the window was something unfamiliar. A box of black, sugared fruit. Were they prunes, we asked the lady in charge of the shop. No, they were *noci candite*, candied walnuts. Gathered green, we were told, they turn black and soft when preserved – like our own pickled walnuts, but there the resemblance ends – and as we saw them there in their frilly paper cases they looked like nuggets of onyx, sugar-dusted. They were about the size of damsons, soft, clove-scented; and, we learned, they were a speciality unique to this one particular Turin sweetshop. To this day I remember that it was called Cotto, and was – I hope still is – at No. 68. The lady, who turned out to be the owner, told us that the recipe for the *noci candite* had long ago been brought to Cotto's by a confectioner from the Asti region of Piedmont – perhaps as far back as the days when Turin was the capital of the old Duchy of Savoy.

That year I took home several boxes of Cotto candied walnuts for Christmas presents – and every autumn for several years to come I wrote to Turin for a new supply of the Cotto candied walnuts.

From *Italian Food*, ELIZABETH DAVID

It was the Great Masten who had the house built, at the end of the eighteenth century, when he became a *particulare*, a man who had land of his own, oxen, cows, chickens and rabbits, and so many acres that he had to hire extra hands. He was in a hurry and he didn't bother much about the foundations even though the house, with its yellowish facade, was anchored to the ground through the years, the long sequence of rooms, one after the other. A building of two storeys plus the attic with its low windows directly under the roof. The brick path ran from the house to the driveway that curved down towards the gate, while the barn and the stables extended from one side until they reached the road where the great wooden gate opened. There is no knowing what that road was called then; the house was the last in the town and, later, when another was built, it was on condition that there be a blind wall between it and the Great Masten's garden.

No one has ever found out the Great Masten's real name because the parish registers were burned during the first Napoleonic campaign. No doubt, he was a man who had grown rich thanks to the comings and goings of soldiers, providing fodder for the horses and grain, first hidden, then sold for three times its value. And wine to get French and Austrians drunk, and Russians and Bavarians, Alsatians, during those endless wars that had coloured as in a game of exchanges, the map of central Europe. All we know of him is that, working from sunrise to sundown, never letting up, in a few years he doubled the acreage, and that his legs were so long he could step across ditches without jumping. He married late, and of the many children he brought into the world only two sons grew to manhood: Pietro and Giuseppe. Pietro, known as Pidrèn, was later nicknamed Sacarlott. Giuseppe, on the other hand, was so blond that, from childhood, he was called Giai, which in dialect means yellow.

His wife went first to join all those dead babies, buried in haste to the sound of the Tribundina, with a plain stone to indicate where. He, the Great Masten, fell under the heels of a wagon one summer when the rain poured down so heavily that the Tanaro overflowed its banks and the fields were flooded

before the corn had been harvested. They didn't even have time
to toll the Agony, and during the funeral it went on raining and
the relatives had to take shelter inside the Church. The hail
shattered a stained-glass window. Pidrèn and Giai decided to
marry: they were twenty-two and twenty-one respectively.

A cousin, known as Mandrognin, told them about two
young sisters who would also be good company for each other
in the house. Two girls from Moncalvo whose mother was dead;
they embroidered hangings and vestments for the church and
sometimes, seated at the cushion bristling with pins, they
worked at lace-making under the strict surveillance of an aunt
from the Veneto, Luison. One of the girls, Maria, was a
brunette; the other had that dull brown hair that some women
try in vain to pass off as blonde. A colour so common in certain
parts of the Monferrato region that it almost suggests an adap-
tation of the species: the colour of the land, the mud, the
interminable mists.

The brunette, Maria, was beautiful; Matelda, on the contrary, her eyelids always lowered, talked with plants and seeds;
and the vestments she embroidered were the most prized in all
Moncalvo. On solemn occasions, when the priest held up the
chalice, glints of purple and gold darted from the embroidered
silk on his back. Some even said that Matelda talked with ants
and, on certain evenings, with her Guardian Angel.

Pidrèn and Giai both fell in love with Maria. They called in
a painter, to decorate the ceiling of the living-room with four
different views; in the other rooms they were satisfied with a few
scrolls that might please the girls from Moncalvo. They planted
a walnut, two pears, and some rusmeni, rust-apples. The walnut

grew until it cast too much shadow on the house and was later decapitated; then it spread out like a gigantic umbrella and became the focal point of the garden.

The dark girl from Moncalvo chose the younger of the brothers, Giai. And Pidrèn, who should have taken Matelda, went off in the train of a young French general, who was beginning a brilliant career in Italy. Ah, he's a *testa mata*, that Pidrèn, a strange one, refusing that Matelda, who, when she holds her needle, has the Madonna at her feet . . . and he'd rather go off with that Frenchman, that *Bonaparti* . . . But Matelda, who was embroidering an altar cloth covered with flowers and birds, and violet-winged butterflies, waited. Perhaps some voice, not entirely of this world, had advised her to be patient.

From *The Dust Roads of Monferrato*, ROSETTA LOY

Monday (11 October 1897)
Villa Giudice, Posilippo

The Neapolitan papers have turned out to be the worst form of American journalism. They fill columns with me, and write interviews of a fictitious character. I wish the world would let me alone, and really I thought that at Naples I would be at peace. I dare say they will tire of this nonsense soon.

I hope you will do a good thing with Aphrodite, and that when you make lots of money, you will be able to find time to come to Naples, which I know you would like. The museum is full, as you know, of lovely Greek bronzes. The only bother is that they all walk about the town at night.

However, one gets delicately accustomed to that – and there are compensations. Ever yours

OSCAR WILDE (letter to Ernest Dowson)

Thursday (21 October 1897)
Villa Giudice, Posilippo

My dear Stanley, You have borne my bomb-shell with sweetness of temper and delightful resignation: I felt sure you would . . .

I am awaiting type-written proofs of my poem from Smithers, after which I hope in a short time to see it published. I am also supervising an Italian version of Salome, which is being made here by a young Neapolitan poet. I hope to produce it on the stage here, if I can find an actress of troubling beauty and flute-like voice. Unfortunately most of the tragic actresses of Italy – with the exception of Duse – are stout ladies, and I don't think I could bear a stout Salome.

Pray remember me to Oswald, and believe me, sincerely yours

OSCAR WILDE (letter to Stanley V. Makower)

SEGALAVECCHIA

Halfway through Lent the children and young ones would go round the houses carrying a representation of Segalavecchia. Despite my protestations, that year too I accepted my usual role of the old woman and of the oak tree, even if, at 20, I seemed a little old for their childish pranks.

Segalavecchia is an ancient tradition which celebrates the death of winter and the birth of spring. It starts by going round the village banging on the doors, everybody goes into the house accompanied by accordion music, singing this song, 'Be happy country folk, now the axemen have arrived, if the boss lends us the house we'll chop the old woman down!'

We were always greeted warmly, people waited for us happy and excited with a few glasses of good wine in their stomachs.

'Sir Nicola' was played by Severino di Sforna, who had that air of a nobleman about him, he even spoke with a soft R; he wore a *blouson* jacket, a large straw boater and had his cheeks painted red. I went in with him, covered from head to toe and rolled up in rags because at the beginning I had to resemble an old oak tree. Then 'the Meddler' barges in, he who never misses a trick, has little desire to work, is a gossip and an interferer, always ready to tell the others what should be done.

At a certain point the boss decides that it is time to chop down the old oak tree and has the axemen called. They soon arrive, axes at the ready, bold and eager. Usually one of the two is half drunk and, with his antics, starts to entertain the spectators, while the other tries in vain to bring down the oak. The 'killer' enters, all dressed in black, having his fun scaring the women and children. In the end he plunges his knife into the tree, which finally gives way and falls to the hard earth. And so begins the transformation of tree to old woman.

Who knows why the story is told in this way? Anyway it's always been like that so there's little that's worth philosophising over.

A little later the stooping old man arrives wearing a fake beard and a battered old hat back-to-front, searching for his old wife who had disappeared after one of their usual arguments. He is as deaf as a post and showing signs of late senile dementia. He finds his wife stretched out on the ground and hurries away to call 'Doctor Sbrodola' and 'Nurse Grullo' who then arrive to a fanfare on the back of an old ass who was always played by Checco del Chivrulla, given that the poor thing could bray like a beauty! The two begin to shell out diagnoses here and there and begin a somewhat complicated surgical procedure. There is much cackling, especially when they begin to pull out every kind of object imaginable from the woman's stomach: a string of sausages, a cuckoo clock, a gigantic bra, a who-knows-what in the shape of a cucumber, and so on. After a while the little old lady stretches out her rickety old legs and dies! Someone runs to call 'Don Fasullo' the priest and 'Fiacca' the altar-boy, who is the funniest of all the characters: he was called Peppino dei Trinari, a redhead, drier than a dried fig and covered in freckles. He wore a flame red garment with a white overcoat and was everybody's favourite, winking at the girls being his speciality.

Then begin the ceremonies and the prayers and the priest starts the blessings right and left, spraying holy water – or who knows what else – amongst the screams of the women and the jumps of the fleeing children.

When the moment came for the 'police' to arrive, I was still stretched out on the floor, bored of doing so even though it seemed funny seeing everybody's faces from down below.

After the ridiculous enquiries, the farce ends with the 'killer's' arrest and finally the group sings its chorus accompanied by the accordion, the farewell song, dancing and going round with out caps outstretched collecting coins and eggs. 'Please excuse us good folks, if we have disturbed your sleep, we must be going now.'

Inside those houses there was such a joyous atmosphere that on reflection I rather regret it. We felt like friends, good countryfolk, all the envy, insults, grief and fatigue were forgotten. We really tried to bury the worst of ourselves together with the final frosts and to baptise with joy the new season. Even ridiculing those who made us suffer, like the landlord, the policeman, the doctor and, at the end, the priest, gave you a satisfaction like kicking your enemy's dog up the arse!

But what's more, Segalavecchia often served as a birth-place for certain pleasantries: it was a good excuse for entering the houses and maybe finding a girl that you really liked.

That year, among the other stop-offs, they decided to pass by Mr Vincenzo's house. I began to feel nervous: inside I felt the embarrassment and fear of meeting Rosa there, where she lived, of letting her think that I was just a little boy.

The house was on two floors in the middle of the village and the entrance was up a very narrow staircase. Mr Vincenzo lived on the first floor, while she, with her two children – a 10-year-old girl and a 6-year-old boy – had settled into their new home on the second floor where the granary used to be.

We knocked, they opened the door, there was the usual revelry and the play began.

The two children were quite scared; I remember that she kept them near to her, sometimes they laughed a little, but often they hid behind their hands; even she was not familiar with our customs and seemed perplexed in the midst of all the village folk who had run up to Mr Vincenzo's so as not to miss the Segalavecchia.

Fortunately, I was bandaged up to such an extent that I was hardly recognisable.

Everything went along fine. The atmosphere was warming up and out of the corner of my eyes, lying down there on the ground, I was enjoying Rosa's laugh, that gracious gesture of covering her mouth with her hand, of bending forward and shaking her curly head; of kissing her children's heads and chattering lovingly with them.

The worst came when 'the priest' entered.

Just at that point the onlookers were all huddled around us. Rosa was just a few centimetres from where I was lying on the ground. When Don Fasullo took to spraying the holy water, she began to scream and laugh and made a sudden leap into the air, passing right in front of my upturned face. It was only a second, an image so quick it could have been a mere suspicion. But it will remain in my eyes like the magnesium flash lamp of a photographer. As she leapt I got a good look under her long skirt: she was wearing black wool stockings supported by elastic just above the knees, she had slender smooth thighs, white like mother of pearl. But above all else . . . Good God – she wasn't wearing any knickers!

In that roguish leap, agile and playful, I just saw her small dark thing for a split second, but I could almost smell it!

And yes, I saw it well.

It was like a fire had broken out inside me, agitation took over me, a desire, a hot-sweat so that I couldn't stay still any longer.

What's more, as I was making my escape she recognised me and smiled me her sweet flirtation. 'Mind . . . !' she said in a gesture. I was confounded.

GRAPE HARVEST

I could almost hear the sounds of the wine cellars when, about a fortnight before the grape harvest, they started to wash the casks. To my ear, each one had a different tone depending on the type of wood, the age, the size, the way it was made; they were like the notes of a drum which resonates under the wooden mallets or beats of hands, voices which wake you up after a long silence. They would send a small boy into the bigger casks to scrape away the dregs. For the children it seemed like a game, like the game of rolling the smaller barrels whilst inside them. They were washed with boiling water steeped in peach and nut leaves.

On the first day of the grape harvest everyone – male, female, old and young – began with a breakfast of stewed dried salt cod in tomato sauce flavoured with raisins or dried plums. We would leave between nine and ten, when it was beginning to get hot, behind us the people carrying shears, baskets and gangplanks. A line of tubs made its way along the rows of vines; the baskets filled with grapes were emptied out one after the other into the tubs; when they were full as a pregnant woman, we left the cart to go back to the wine store.

I liked to do the most tiring jobs. I confess it: partly out of vanity, so I could congratulate myself, but partly in order to thank God for the strength he has given me and to save exhausting those older than me who already had much drudgery in their lives.

In those days we were in the fields up until the last glimmers of light disappeared, then we would all assemble in the wine store. The darkness came down unexpectedly, a soft, dark substance, soaked in the sweetish smell of grapes. A smell which already spoke of fires and rain, of chestnuts and of waiting. You heard the carts struggling to assemble themselves outside, their wheels making tracks in the mud formed by the first squalls of rain, the strained panting of the animals and the excited voices of the harvesters.

All the grapes were tipped into the presses, and then the most playful part of the work began: the crushing. We took off our shoes and washed our feet thoroughly, and then jumped inside as if for a dance. There was great excitement everywhere, partly because the women had to pull their skirts up above their knees, and in those days, a bare leg was something you certainly didn't see everyday!

We would carry on tramping up and down until late into the night, leaping over each other doing pirouettes, which sometimes also caused accidents. Towards midnight the women brought a stack, the last cut of ham, grilled herring, still-warm cakes.

I cannot explain how great was the satisfaction of tasting the wine once it had matured, of tasting the fruit of our precise and exhausting labour, subject to the caprices of the weather and the games of the moon. It was as if some people could almost speak with the wine; just after one mouthful they could tell you its entire story, its life as it were.

From *Under a Distant Sky*, MARCO RUFINI

[Leonardo da Vinci was] specially endowed by the hand of God himself . . . this was seen and acknowledged by all men . . . His gifts were such that his fame extended far and wide and he was held in the highest estimation not only in his own time, but also, and even to a greater extent, after his death; and this will continue to be in all succeeding ages. Truly wonderful indeed and divinely gifted was Leonardo da Vinci.

From *The Lives of the Artists*, GIORGIO VASARI

CHRIST STOPPED AT EBOLI

Many years have gone by, years of war and of what men call History. Buffeted here and there at random I have not been able to return to my peasants as I promised when I left them, and I do not know when, if ever, I can keep my promise. But closed in one room, in a world apart, I am glad to travel in my memory to that other world, hedged in by custom and sorrow, cut off from History and the State, eternally patient, to that land without comfort or solace, where the peasant lives out his motionless civilization on barren ground in remote poverty, and in the presence of death.

'We're not Christians,' they say. 'Christ stopped short of here, at Eboli.' 'Christian' in their way of speaking means 'human being,' and this almost proverbial phrase that I have so often heard them repeat may be no more than the expression of a hopeless feeling of inferiority. We're not Christians, we're not human beings; we're not thought of as men but simply as beasts, beasts of burden, or even less than beasts, mere creatures of the wild. They at least live for better or for worse, like angels or demons, in a world of their own, while we have to submit to the world of Christians, beyond the horizon, to carry its weight and to stand comparison with it. But the phrase has a much deeper meaning and, as is the way of symbols, this is the literal one. Christ did stop at Eboli, where the road and the railway leave the coast of Salerno and turn into the desolate reaches of Lucania. Christ never came this far, nor did time, nor the individual soul, nor hope, nor the relation of cause to effect, nor reason nor history. Christ never came; just as the Romans never came, content to garrison the highways without penetrating the mountains and forests, nor the Greeks, who flourished beside the Gulf of Taranto. None of the pioneers of Western civilization brought here his sense of the passage of time, his deification of the State or that ceaseless activity which feeds upon itself. No one has come to this land except as an enemy, a conqueror, or a visitor devoid of understanding. The seasons pass to-day over the toil of the peasants, just as they did three thousand years before Christ; no message, human or divine, has reached this stubborn poverty. We speak a different language, and here our tongue is incomprehensible. The greatest travellers have not gone beyond the limits of their own world; they have trodden the paths of their own souls, of good and evil, of morality and redemption. Christ descended into the underground hell of Hebrew moral principle in order to break down its doors in time and to seal them up into eternity. But to this shadowy land, that knows neither sin nor redemption from sin, where evil is not moral but is only the pain residing forever in earthly things, Christ did not come. Christ stopped at Eboli.

CARLO LEVI

THE MOON AND THE BONFIRE

Last year, the first time I came back to the village, I went almost stealthily to look at the hazels again. The hill at Gaminella was a long slope covered as far as the eye could see with vineyards and terraces, a slant so gradual that if you looked up you could not see the top – and on the top, somewhere, there are other vineyards and other woods and paths – this hill, then, looked as if it had been flayed by the winter and showed up the bareness of the earth and of the tree trunks. In the wintry light I saw its great mass falling gradually away towards Canelli, where our valley finishes. Along the rough country road which follows the Belbo I came to the parapet of the little bridge and to the reed-bed. I saw on the bank of the wall of the cottage with its huge blackened stones, the twisted fig-tree and the gaping window and I thought of the terrible winters there. But round about it the face of the land and the trees were changed; the clump of hazels had disappeared and our closely cut patch of millet grass grown smaller. From the byre an ox lowed and in the cold evening air I smelt the manure heap. So the man who had the croft now was not so badly off as we had been. I had always expected something like this or perhaps even that the cottage would have collapsed; I had imagined myself so often on the parapet of the bridge wondering how I could possibly have spent so many years in this hole, walking these few paths, taking the goat to pasture and looking for apples which had rolled down the bank, sure that the world ended where the road overhung the Belbo. But I had not expected not to find the hazels any more. That was the end of everything. These changes made me so cast down that I didn't call out or go on to the threshing floor. There and then I understood what it meant not to be born in a place, not to have it in my blood and be already half-buried there along with my forebears so that any change of crops didn't matter much. Of course there were some clumps of the same hazels on the hillsides and I could still find them, but if I had been the owner of this stretch of river bank I would rather have cleared it and sown it with grain; as it was, it had the same effect on me as those rooms you rent in the city, where you live for a day – or for a year – and then when you move on they stay bare and empty shells; they are not really yours, they are dead.

It was a good job that in the evening I turned my back on Gaminella and had in front of me the ridges of the hill at Salto on the other side of the Belbo with its broad meadows which tapered away towards the summit. And lower on this hill, too, there were stretches of trees, and the paths and the scattered farms were there as I had seen them day in, day out, year in, year out, sitting on the beam behind the cottage or on the parapet of the bridge.

Then all these years until I was called up – when I was a hand on the farm they call La Mora, in the rich plain beyond Belbo, and when Padrino had sold his croft at Gaminella and gone with the girls to Cossano – I had only to raise my eyes from the fields to see the vineyards high up on Salto and the way they sloped gradually down towards Canelli, towards the railway and the whistle of the train which ran along by the Belbo morning and evening, making me think of wonders, of stations and cities.

Thus it was that for a long time I thought this village where I had not been born was the whole world. Now that I have really seen the world and know that it is made up of a whole lot of little villages, I am not sure that I was so far wrong when I was a boy. You wander over land and sea just as the lads who were young with me used to go to the festas in the villages round about and dance and drink and fight and bring home flags and barked knuckles. Or you grow grapes and sell them at Canelli; or gather truffles and take them to Alba. There is Nuto, my friend from Salto, who supplies all the valley as far as Cannio with wooden buckets and wine-presses. What does it all mean then? That you need a village, if only for the pleasure of leaving it. Your own village means that you are not alone, that you know there's something of you in the people and the plants and the soil, that even when you are not there it waits to welcome you. But it isn't easy to stay there quietly. For a year now

I have had an eye on it and have taken a trip out there from Genoa whenever I could; but it still evades me. Time and experience teach you these things. Is it possible that at forty, after all my travelling, I still don't know what it is to have a village?

There's one thing I can't get used to. Everyone here thinks I have come back to buy a house for myself and they call me the American and show off their daughters. This ought to please a man who left without even a name, and indeed it does. But it isn't enough. I like Genoa, too; I like to know that the world is round, and to have one foot on the gangway. From the time when, as a boy, I leant on my spade at the farm-gate at La Mora and listened to the chatter of people who had nothing better to do as they passed by on the main road – ever since that time, for me, the little hills round Canelli are doors opening on the world. Nuto, who, compared with me, has never been far from Salto, says that if you want to make a life of it in the valley you mustn't ever leave it. Yet he's the one who, when he was still a young lad, got the length of playing the clarinet in the band beyond Canelli and as far away even as Spigno and Ovcada, over there where the sun rises. We speak about it from time to time and he laughs.

CESARE PAVESE

J. M. W. T*URNER*

Like Aeneas, Turner finally found Italy. As we have seen, he had been painting Italy before he got there: classical ruins; homages to Claude; and tributes to Richard Wilson, such as *Diana and Callisto* of 1796 and *Tivoli and the Roman Campagna, after Wilson* of 1798. He had wanted to go to Italy in 1816 and expressed his disappointment when he told Holworthy that, as well as Yorkshire being soaked with rain, Italy was 'deluged, Switzerland a wash-pot . . . [and] all chance of getting over the Simplon or any of the other passes now vanished like the morning mist.' Italy stayed in his mind as he read Byron's poetry and copied bits of the Reverend J.J. Eustace's *Tour through Italy* of 1813 and made commissioned watercolours to be engraved for James Hakewill's *Picturesque Tour of Italy*. One might have thought, from a watercolour he did in 1817, that he had already been there. The watercolour, which Fawkes bought, showed Vesuvius erupting, full of fire and colour, though it was based on someone else's drawing.

Turner – now forty-four – had [already] decided to go. He set off on the last day of July 1819.

Early starts, long days in the coaches; bad inns, poor food, awful beds. But the Alps, wonderful as ever, always allowed one to encounter what Byron called 'throned Eternity in icy halls/Of cold Sublimity'. Then down to Lake Como, Milan, Verona and Venice – drawing, drawing, drawing during his short stay there. On to Bologna, Rimini, Ancona and over the Apennines – the further south, the more brilliant the light – sketching the streets, squares and gateways of the towns, his fellow-travellers waiting for a diligence or *vettura*, the hillsides with villages or towers. South of Ancona he noted among his sketches colours that reminded him of his heroes: . . . 'color of the Hill Wilson Claude the olives the light of these when the

Sun shone grey [turn]ing the Ground redish green Gray
now . . . to Purple the Sea quite Blue, under the Sun a Warm
vapour from the Sun Bluer relieving the Shadows of the Olive
Tree dark while the foliage Light or the whole when in shadow
a quiet Grey. Beautiful dark Green yet warm, the middle Trees
get Bluish in parts for distance, the aquaduct redish the foreground Light grey in shadow'.

Now that the long wars were over, Rome was once again luring
many foreign artists as visitors and residents, particularly the
English and Germans. But Turner was his usual somewhat
secretive self, staying in the Palazzo Poli and quietly getting on
with the job. From the moment he arrived he was out sketching
the ruins and prospects of the city from the various vantage
points; he drew the works of art, statues as well as painting.
From the Palazzo Poli, he sketched the extravagantly Baroque
Fontana de Trevi with its gods and sea monsters. He deter-
minedly filled sketchbook after sketchbook; he made several
hundred larger drawings. His friend Chantrey was also in town,
as fond of society as ever, and rather worried because Turner was
being stand-offish – Chantrey didn't know where Turner was
lodging. However, he was seen at the Venetian Academy of
Painting in Rome on 15 November. Moore, the poet, also went,
with the fashionable sculptor Canova, and later in the day at the
Academy of St Luke, where Canova had put him up for honorary membership, albeit in his letter of recommendation
spelling his name 'Touner.' Lawrence had written to Canova to
introduce Turner – England's 'finest landscape painter' – and
asked Canova to be patient, as Turner was 'unacquainted with

the Italian language'. Lawrence, Turner and Canova shared an interest in the Venetian masters Titian, Tintoretto and Veronese – though ultimately Turner preferred Tintoretto.

Turner was spotted on the tower of the Capitol one stormy day when the Princess of Denmark and a friend of Moore's named Colonel Camac were also sightseeing there. The Colonel noticed that the wind was bothering the Princess and plucked Turner's umbrella from under his arm to shelter the Princess. The umbrella was blown inside out, breaking some of its ribs. The Princess smiled her thanks to the Colonel; Turner scowled. He had presumably been disturbed when sketching *and* had his umbrella wrecked. There were further sightings of him in Naples, to which he had dashed in hopes of observing Vesuvius erupting – the real as opposed to the imaginary thing. One of Sir John Soane's sons, then in Italy, wrote home to his father, 'Turner is in the neighbourhood of Naples making rough pencil sketches to the astonishment of the fashionables, who wonder what use these rough drafts can be – simple souls!'

Any who thought the taciturn Turner would enliven the social scene in Rome soon changed their minds. Hazlitt called Rome 'of all places the worse to study in', and Turner did not want the city's distractions.

Lord Byron was in Rome – a friend of the poet Thomas Moore and acquainted with Samuel Rogers, the London banker and versifier, whom Turner knew – but there is no record of a meeting between the fashionable, unconventional poet and the moody, unconventional painter. The fourth Italy-centred canto of Byron's world-weary epic *Childe Harold* had been published in 1818, and Turner read it. He owed to Byron the lines adapted from *Childe Harold III* he attached to his *Field of Waterloo*, shown at the RA in 1818. Byron's work became part of the filter through which his mind sieved his Italian experience. Shelley's work seems to have performed a similar function. 'Ode to the West Wind' was written at this time and that poet's almost tactile reaction to the time-wrecked beauty of the Italian coast was much like his own.

From *Standing in the Sun, A Life of J.M.W. Turner*, ANTONY BAILEY

ITALIAN JOURNEYS

Milan, what is more, has a railway station. Actually it is not a railway station, but *the* railway station. There are other stations in Milan – sixteen to be precise, not to speak of an entire underground system – but Milano Centrale is The One, ultimate in the majesty of its affirmations, in its profligate splendour of revealed possibility, in its eternal defiance of all those curmudgeonly, mean-spirited, joyless, inhuman, godforsaken community-haters who tell us that train travel is dead and that our aspirations should soar no higher than the private car.

Milano Centrale sets at nought such banal individualism. Its monstrousness reduces human self-consequence to something quintessentially ephemeral. Its scale is so huge, the terms in which it engages with our experience so apparently limitless, that it does not specially care whether we get to the end of out ticket queues, whether (a frequent dilemma, this, in Italy) we have the correct sprinkling of small coins to please the philosophically glum clerks at the windows, or whether we shall catch the train with whose existence the capricious indicator board at the entrance to the platform persists in teasing us.

For sheer moral education there are few places like it on earth. It forces an existential crisis on the traveller by the tricks it plays with the rhetoric of architecture. The spaces within its great sequences of booking halls are archaic in their immensity; whole villages might be crammed into them without squalor or discomfort. Stairs and escalators hurl you up into the realm of an unknown actuality, but even these seem emblematic, ghastly metaphors of ill-judged optimism. For halfway up is a little set of marble terraces, on whose stone benches sit or lie those who, for whatever reason, have abandoned the delusive ascent. The poorest of students, with grubby feet and matted hair, their lean bodies burned black, their eyes as visionary with hunger and thirst as those of desert hermits, sprawl beside Calabrian families picnicking off peppery sausage and coarse bread washed down with swigs of wine dark as cuttlefish ink. Pink-shouldered northern girls from a country where the sun is a cheese tied up in a muslin bag scribble their postcards next to snoring nondescripts wrapped in clothes whose true shape and colours vanished aeons ago. These are the sirens and lotus-eaters and Circean beasts of Milano Centrale, wheedling you to turn back, not to bother with the hopeless business of going on.

They are right, of course, for at the head of the stairs, in the vast grey gallery with its coffered ceiling and mosaic floor, a man might comfortably pass the remainder of his life. There's a kind of malaise bred in railway stations – and, I grudgingly concede, at airports – which makes you terrified of leaving them for fear of the complexities lying in ambush beyond. Thus, I am convinced, there must be a kind of alternative parasitic community living in Milan station which manages to avoid every attempt by the authorities to dislodge it, perhaps not unlike those peasant families whom Tsar Alexander II discovered existing, complete with their cows, in the attics of the Winter Palace in St Petersburg. Why should anybody want to get out? There are two cafes, five bookstalls, a shop selling designer clothes, a bank and a chemist's and an exceedingly smart lavatory. There are a chapel and waxwork museum and one of those admirable Italian institutions known as *albergo diurno*, in which the traveller, on payment of a modest fee, may take a shower, have a bath, lie down for an hour or two, get his shoes shined and his hair cut and generally be made presentable to the world. And there is the cavernously dismal cafeteria, almost always empty except for an unshaven Sicilian, a baglady in animated conversation with herself, and me, which serves the very worst food in Italy.

Buildings like this induce a kind of insanity. It was erected under fascism, a fact which no sensitive observer can ignore, even without the lictors' axes and gung-ho cracker-mottoes of Mussolinian wisdom which adorned it in the bad old times. Inherent in all political ideologies is a lethal element of fatuity which has much to do with the absence, in most politicians, of any redeeming sense of the ridiculous. Among the many reasons why Italians have not yet managed to come to terms with the experience of fascism must surely be a simple embarrassment at the barking absurdity of it all; considered in this light, Milano Centrale, as an essay in crushing, get-this, look-at-me triumphalism, is devastatingly silly. Its mock-Roman bas-reliefs (including a Rape of the Sabines which says everything meant by the Italian word *convincente* – rather more than just convincing), its cliffs of marble and granite and basalt, its great mottled plains of tessellated paving, have the imbecile musclebound grotesqueness of some steroid-popping Mister Universe.

It is this sense of exaggerated contour, of unsustainable weights and unbridgeable gulfs, which must in the end impel the traveller towards escape. The intrinsic romance of the place lies in the drama of release in which it encourages one to take part. To anybody with the merest jot of an associative faculty, the names on the yellow *Partenze* lists are instant spurs to a restless imagination. Suddenly you are Byron's Childe Harold or his musical alter ego, Berlioz's Harold in Italy, or you are the wandering Goethe of Tischbein's splendid portrait – 'I slipped out of Carlsbad at three in the morning' – or the Président de Brosses or Augustus J.C. Hare or Corot or Claude, or anybody else who has imbued themselves memorably in the experience of Italy, and here at once for the taking are the great reverberative toponyms: Venice, Florence, Padua, Vicenza, Genoa, Turin, Rome, Naples, even the promise of distant Sicily.

JONATHAN KEATES

There is not in Italy, they say (and I believe them), a lovelier residence than the Palazzo Peschiere, or Palace of the Fishponds, whither we removed as soon as our three months' tenancy of the Pink Jail at Albaro had ceased and determined.

It stands on a height within the walls of Genoa but aloof from the town; surrounded by beautiful gardens of its own, adorned with statues, vases, fountains, marble basins, terraces, walks of orange-trees and lemon-trees, groves of roses and camellias. All its apartments are beautiful in their proportions and decorations; but the great hall, some fifty feet in height, with three large windows at the end overlooking the whole town of Genoa, the harbour, and the neighbouring sea, affords one of the most fascinating and delightful prospects in the world. Any house more cheerful and habitable than the great rooms are, within, it would be difficult to conceive, and certainly nothing more delicious than the scene without, in sunshine or in moonlight, could be imagined. It is more like an enchanted place in an Eastern story than a grave and sober lodging.

In Genoa, and thereabouts, they train the vines on trellis-work supported on square clumsy pillars, which, in themselves, are anything but picturesque. But, here, they twine them around trees, and let them trail along the hedges; and the vine-yards are full of trees regularly planted for this purpose, each with its own vine twining and clustering about it. Their leaves are now of the brightest gold and deepest red; and never was anything so enchantingly graceful and full of beauty. Through miles of these delightful forms and colours, the road winds its way. The wild festoons, the elegant wreaths and crowns, and garlands of all shapes; the fairy nets flung over great trees, and making them prisoners in sort; the tumbled heaps and mounds of exquisite shapes upon the ground; how rich and beautiful they are! And every now and then, a long line of trees will be all bound and garlanded together; as if they had taken hold of one another and were coming dancing down the field!

Parma has cheerful, stirring streets for an Italian town and, consequently, is not so characteristic as many places of less note. Always excepting the retired Piazza, where the Cathedral, Baptistry, and Campanile – ancient buildings, of a sombre brown, embellished with innumerable grotesque monsters and dreamy-looking creatures carved in marble and red stone – are clustered in a noble and magnificent repose. Their silent presence was only invaded, when I saw them, by the twittering of the many birds that were flying in and out of the crevices in the stones and little nooks in the architecture where they had made their nests. They were busy, rising from the cold shade of Temples made with hands, into the sunny air of Heaven. Not so the worshippers within, who were listening to the same drowsy chaunt, or kneeling before the same kinds of images and tapers, or whispering, with their heads down, in the self-same dark confessionals, as I had left in Genoa and everywhere else.

The decayed and mutilated paintings with which this church was covered, have, to my thinking, a remarkably mournful and depressing influence. It is miserable to see great works of art – something of the souls of Painters – perishing and fading away, like human forms. This cathedral is odorous with the rotting of Correggio's frescos in the Cupola. Heaven knows how beautiful they may have been at one time. Connoisseurs fall into raptures with them now; but such a labyrinth of arms and legs; such heaps of foreshortened limbs, entangled and involved and jumbled together: no operative surgeon, gone mad, could imagine in his wildest delirium.

There is a very interesting subterranean church here: the roof supported by marble pillars, behind each of which there seemed to be at least one beggar in ambush: to say nothing of the tombs and secluded altars. From every one of these lurking places, such crowds of phantom-looking men and women, leading other men and women with twisted limbs, or chattering jaws, or paralytic gestures, or idiotic heads, or some other sad infirmity, came hobbling out to beg, that if the ruined frescos in the cathedral above had been suddenly animated, and had retired to this lower church, they could hardly have made a greater confusion, or exhibited a more confounding display of arms and legs.

There is Petrarch's Monument, too; and there is the Baptistry, with its beautiful arches and immense font; and there is a gallery containing some very remarkable pictures, whereof a few were being copied by hairy-faced artists, with little velvet caps, more off their heads than on. There is the Farnese Palace, too; and in one of the dreariest spectacles of decay that ever was seen – a grand, old, gloomy theatre, mouldering away.

It was most delicious weather when we came into Modena where the darkness of the sombre colonnades over the footways skirting the main street on either side, was made refreshing and agreeable by the bright sky, so wonderfully blue. I passed from all the glory of the day, into a dim cathedral.

Again, an ancient sombre town, under the brilliant sky, with heavy arcades over the footways of the older streets, and light and more cheerful archways in the newer portions of the town. Again, brown piles of sacred buildings, with more birds flying in and out of chinks in the stones; and more snarling monsters for the base of the pillars. Again, rich churches, drowsy Masses, curling incense, tinkling bells, priests in bright vestments, pictures, tapers, lace altar cloths, crosses, images, and artificial flowers.

There is a grave and learned air about the city, and a pleasant gloom upon it, that would leave it, a distinct and separate impression in the mind, among a crowd of cities, though it were not still further marked in the traveller's remembrance by the two brick leaning towers (sufficiently unsightly in themselves, it must be acknowledged) inclining cross-wise as if they were bowing stiffly to each other – a most extraordinary termination to the perspective of some of the narrow streets.

Bologna, being very full of tourists detained there by an inundation which rendered the road to Florence impassable, I was quartered up at the top of an hotel, in an out-of-the-way road which I never could find; containing a bed, big enough for a boarding school, which I couldn't fall asleep in. The chief among the waiters who visited this lonely retreat, where there was no other company but the swallows in the broad eaves over the window, was a man of one idea in connection with England; and the subject of this harmless monomania was Lord Byron. I made the discovery by accidentally remarking to him at breakfast that the matting with which the floor was covered was very comfortable at that season, when he immediately replied that Milor Beeron had been much attached to that kind of matting. Observing, at the same moment, that I took no milk, he exclaimed with enthusiasm, that Milor Beeron had never touched it. At first, I took it for granted, in my innocence, that he had been one of the Beeron servants; but no, he said, no, he was in the habit of speaking about my Lord, to English gentlemen; that was all. He knew all about him, he said. In proof of it, he connected him with every possible topic, from the Monte Pulciano wine at dinner (which was grown on an estate he had owned), to the big bed itself, which was the very model of his. When I left the inn, he coupled with his final bow in the yard, a parting assurance that the road by which I was going, had been Milor Beeron's favourite ride; and before the horse's feet had well begun to clatter on the pavement, he ran briskly upstairs again, I dare say to tell some other Englishman in some other solitary room that the guest who had just departed was Lord Beeron's living image.

I had been half afraid to go to Verona, lest it should at all put me out of conceit with Romeo and Juliet. But, I was no sooner come into the old market-place, than the misgiving vanished. It is so fanciful, quaint, and picturesque a place, formed by such an extraordinary and rich variety of fantastic buildings, that there could be nothing better at the core of even this romantic town: scene of one of the most romantic and beautiful of stories.

It was natural enough to go straight from the Market-place to the House of the Capulets, now degenerated into a most miserable little inn. Noisy *vetterini* and muddy market-carts were disputing possession of the yard, which was ankle-deep in dirt, with a brood of splashed and bespattered geese; and there was a grim-visaged dog, viciously panting in a doorway, who would certainly have had Romeo by the leg, the moment he put it over the wall, if he had existed and been at large in those times. The orchard fell into other hands, and was parted off many years ago; but there used to be one attached to the house – or at all events there may have been – and the hat (Capêllo), the ancient cognizance of the family, may still be seen, carved in stone, over the gateway of the yard.

From Juliet's home, to Juliet's tomb, is a transition as natural to the visitor, as to fair Juliet herself, or to the proudest Juliet that ever has taught the torches to burn bright in any time. So, I went off, with a guide, to an old, old garden, once belonging to an old, old convent, I suppose; and being admitted, at a shattered gate, by a bright-eyed woman who was washing clothes, went down some walks where fresh plants and young flowers were prettily growing among fragments of old wall and ivy-covered mounds; and was shown a little tank, or water-trough, which the bright-eyed woman, drying her arms upon her 'kerchief', called 'La tomba di Giulietta la sfortunáta.' With the best disposition in the world to believe, I could do no more than believe that the bright-eyed woman believed; so I gave her that much credit, and her customary fee in ready money. It was a pleasure, rather than a disappointment, that Juliet's resting-place was forgotten. However consolatory it may have been to Yorick's Ghost, to hear the feet upon the pavement overhead, and, twenty times a day, the repetition of his name, it is better for Juliet to lie out of the track of tourists, and to have no visitors but such as come to graves in springtime, and sweet air, and sunshine.

Pleasant Verona! With its beautiful old palaces, and charming country in the distance seen from terrace walks, and stately, balustraded gardens. With its Roman gates, still spanning the fair street, and casting, in the sunlight of to-day, the shade of fifteen hundred years ago. With its marble-fitted churches, lofty towers, rich architecture, and quaint old quiet thoroughfares, where shouts of Montague and Capulet once resounded.

And made Verona's ancient citizens
Cast by their grave beseeming ornaments,
To wield old partizans.

With its fast-running river, picturesque old bridge, great castle, waving cypresses, and prospect so delightful, and so cheerful! Pleasant Verona!

There is nothing in Italy, more beautiful to me, than the coast-road between Genoa and Spezzia. On one side, sometimes far below, sometimes nearly on a level with the road, and often skirted by rocks of many shapes, there is the free blue sea, with here and there a picturesque felucca gliding slowly on; on the other side are lofty hills, ravines besprinkled with white cottages, patches of dark olive woods, country churches with their light open towers, and country houses gaily painted. On every bank and knoll by the wayside, the wild cactus and aloe flourish in exuberant profusion; and the gardens of the bright villages along the road, are seen, all blushing in the summer-time with clusters of the Belladonna, and are fragrant in the autumn and winter with golden oranges and lemons.

Some of the villages are inhabited, almost exclusively, by fishermen; and it is pleasant to see their great boats drawn up on the beach making little patches of shade, where they lie asleep, or where the women and children sit romping and looking out to sea, while they mend their nets upon the shore.

We came, at dusk, within sight of the Lake of Bolsena, on whose bank there is a little town of the same name, much celebrated for malaria. With the exception of this poor place, there is not a cottage on the banks of the lake, or near it (for nobody dare sleep there); not a boat upon its waters; not a stick or stake to break the dismal monotony of seven-and-twenty watery miles.

A short ride from [another] lake, brought us to Ronciglione, a little town like a large pig-sty, where we passed the night. Next morning at seven o'clock, we started for Rome.

As soon as we were out of the pig-sty, we entered on the Campagna Romana, an undulating flat (as you know), where few people can live; and where, for miles and miles, there is nothing to relieve the terrible monotony and gloom. Of all kinds of country that could, by possibility, lie outside the gates of Rome, this is the aptest and fittest burial-ground for the Dead City. So sad, so quiet, so sullen; so secret in its covering up of great masses of ruin, and hiding them; so like the waste places into which the men possessed with the devil used to go and howl, and rend themselves, in the old days of Jerusalem. We had to traverse thirty miles of this Campagna; and for two-and-twenty we went on and on, seeing nothing but now and than a lonely house, or a villainous-looking shepherd, with matted hair all over his face, and himself wrapped to the chin in a frowsy brown mantle, tending his sheep. At the end of that distance, we stopped to refresh the horses, and to get some lunch, in a common malaria-shaken, despondent little public-house, where every inch of wall and beam, inside, was (according to custom) painted and decorated in a way so miserable that every room looked like the wrong side of another room, and, with its wretched imitation of drapery, and lopsided little daubs of lyres, seemed to have been plundered from behind the scenes of some travelling circus.

When we were fairly going off again, we began, in a perfect fever, to strain our eyes for Rome; and when, after another mile or two, the Eternal City appeared, at length, in the distance; it looked like – I am half afraid to write the word – like LONDON!!! There it lay, under a thick cloud, with innumerable towers, and steeples, and roofs of houses rising up into the sky, and high above them all, one Dome. I swear, that keenly as I felt the absurdity of the comparison, it was so like London, at that distance, that if you could have shown it to me, in a glass, I should have taken it for nothing else.

We entered the Eternal City, at about four o'clock in the afternoon, on the thirtieth of January, by the Porto del Popolo, and came immediately – it was a dark, muddy day, and there had been heavy rain – on the skirts of the Carnival. We did not, then, know that we were only looking at the fag end of the masks, who were driving slowly round and round the Piazza until they could find a promising opportunity for falling into the stream of carriages, and getting, in good time, into the thick of the festivity; and coming among them so abruptly, all travel-stained and weary, was not coming very well prepared to enjoy the scene.

We had crossed the Tiber by the Ponte Molle two or three miles before. It had looked as yellow as it ought to look, and hurrying on between its worn-away and miry banks, had a promising aspect of desolation and ruin. The masquerade dresses on the fringe of the Carnival did great violence to this promise. There were not great ruins, no solemn tokens of antiquity, to be seen; they all lie on the other side of the city. There seemed to be long streets of common-place shops and houses, such as are to be found in any European town; there were busy people, equipages, ordinary walkers to and fro; a multitude of chattering strangers. It was no more *my* Rome; the Rome of anybody's fancy, man or boy, degraded and fallen and lying asleep in the sun among a heap of ruins than the Place de la Concorde in Paris is. A cloudy sky, a dull cold rain, and muddy streets I was prepared for, but not for this, and I confess to having gone to bed, that night, in a very indifferent humour, and with a very considerably quenched enthusiasm.

I think the most popular and most crowded sight (except those of Easter Sunday and Monday, which are open to all classes of people) was the Pope washing the feet of Thirteen men, representing the twelve apostles and Judas Iscariot. The place in which this pious office is performed is one of the chapels of St Peter's, which is gaily decorated for the occasion: the thirteen are sitting, 'all of a row,' on a very high bench, and looking particularly uncomfortable, with the eyes of Heaven knows how many English, French, American, Swiss, Germans, Russians, Swedes, Norwegians, and other foreigners, nailed to their faces all the time. They are robed in white; and on their heads they wear a stiff white cap, like a large English porter-pot, without a handle. Each carries in his hand a nose-gay, of the size of a fine cauliflower; and two of them, on this occasion, wore spectacles which, remembering the characters they sustained, I thought a droll appendage to the costume.

As the two large boxes, appropriate to ladies at this sight, were full to the throat, and getting near was hopeless, we posted off, along with a great crown, to be in time at the Table, where the Pope, in person, waits on these Thirteen; and after a prodigious struggle at the Vatican staircase, and several personal conflicts with the Swiss guard, the whole crowd swept into the room. It was a long gallery hung with drapery of white and red, with another great box for ladies (who are obliged to dress in black at these ceremonies, and to wear black veils), a royal box for the King of Naples and his party; and the table itself, which, set out like a ball supper and ornamented with golden figures of the real apostles, was arranged on an elevated platform on one side of the gallery. The counterfeit apostles' knives and forks were laid out on that side of the table which was nearest to the wall, so that they might be stared at again, without let or hindrance.

The body of the room was full of male strangers; the crowd immense; the heat very great; and the pressure sometimes frightful. It was at its height, when the stream came pouring in, from the feet-washing; and then there were such shrieks and outcries, that a party of Piedmontese dragoons went to the rescue of the Swiss guard, and helped them to calm the tumult.

The ladies were particularly ferocious, in their struggles for places. One lady of my acquaintance was seized round the waist, in the ladies' box, by a strong matron, and hoisted out of her place; and there was another lady (in a back row in the same

box) who improved her position by sticking a large pin into the
ladies before her.

The gentlemen about me were remarkably anxious to see
what was on the table; and one Englishman seemed to have
embarked the whole energy of his nature in the determination
to discover whether there was any mustard.

The apostles and Judas appearing on the platform, after
much expectation, were marshalled, in line, in front of the table,
with Peter at the top; and a good long stare was taken at them
by the company, while twelve of them took a long smell at their
nosegays, and Judas – moving his lips very obtrusively – engaged
in inward prayer. Then, the Pope, clad in a scarlet robe, and
wearing on his head a skull-cap of white satin, appeared in the
midst of a crowd of cardinals and other dignitaries, and took in
his hand a little golden ewer, from which he poured a little
water over one of Peter's hands, while one attendant held a
golden basin; a second, a fine cloth; and a third, Peter's nosegay,
which was taken from him during the operation. This his
Holiness performed, with considerable expedition, on every
man in the line (Judas, I observed, to be particularly overcome
by his condescension); and then the whole Thirteen sat down to
dinner. Grace was said by the Pope. Peter in the chair.

There was white wine, and red wine: and the dinner looked
very good. The courses appeared in portions, one for each apos-
tle: and these being presented to the Pope, by cardinals upon
their knees, were by him handed to the Thirteen. The dishes
appeared to be chiefly composed of fish and vegetables. The
Pope helped the Thirteen to wine also; and, during the whole
dinner, somebody read something aloud, out of a large book –

the Bible, I presume – which nobody could hear, and to which nobody paid the least attention. The Cardinals, and other attendants, smiled to each other . . . as if the thing were a great farce; and if they thought so, there is little doubt they were perfectly right. His Holiness did what he had to do, as a sensible man gets through a troublesome ceremony, and seemed very glad when it was all over.

From *Pictures from Italy*, CHARLES DICKENS

. . . Each time one looks from the windows, steps onto the terrace, a feeling of being suspended, like the white reeling doves, between the mountains and above the sea. This vastness reduces to an intimate size particulars of the landscape – the cypress trees are small as green pen quills; each passing ship could be held in the palm of your hand.

Before dawn, when drooping stars drift at the bedroom window fat as owls, a racket begins along the steep, at moments perilous, path that descends from the mountains. It is the farm families on their way to the marketplace in Taormina. Loose rocks scatter under the stumbling hoofs of overloaded donkeys; there are swells of laughter, a sway of lanterns; it is as though the lanterns were signaling to the far-below night fishermen, who just then are hauling in their nets. Later, in the market, the farmers and the fishermen meet: a small people, not unlike the Japanese, but brawny; indeed there is something almost lush about their lean walnut-hardness. If you question the freshness of a fish, the ripeness of a fig, they are great showmen. *Si Buono.* Your head is pushed down to smell the fish; you are told, with an ecstatic and threatening roll of the eyes how delicious it is. I am always intimidated; not so the villagers, who poke stonily among the tiny jewel tomatoes and never hesitate to sniff a fish or bruise a melon. Shopping, and the arranging of meals, is universally a problem, I know; but after a few months in Sicily even the most skilled householder might consider the noose – no, I exaggerate: the fruit, at least when first it comes into season, is more than excellent; the fish is always good, the *pasta* too. I'm told you can find edible meat; I've never been so fortunate. Also, there is not much choice of vegetables; in winter, eggs are rare. But of course the real trouble is we can't cook; neither, I'm afraid, can our cook. [But] let me tell about the chicken. Not long ago Cecil Beaton, in Sicily on a holiday, came to stay with us. After a few days he was beginning to look a bit peaked: we saw that a more proper effort toward feeding him would have to be made. We sent for a chicken; it appeared, quite alive, and accompanied by the cagey peasant woman who lives slightly higher on the mountain. It was a great black bird – I said it must be very old. No, said the woman, not old, just large. Its neck was wrung, and G., the cook, put it to boil. Around twelve she came to say the chicken was still *troppo duro* – in other words, hard as nails. We advised her to keep trying, and settled on the terrace with glasses of wine, prepared to wait. Several hours, several wine liters later, I went out to the kitchen to find G. in a critical condition: after boiling the chicken, she had roasted it, then fried it and now, in desperation, was giving it another boil. Though there was nothing else to eat, it should never have been brought to the table, for when it was set before us we had to avert our eyes: crowning this steaming heap was the poor bird's severed head, its withered eyes gazing at us, its blackened cockscomb still attached. That evening Cecil, who previously had been staying with other friends on the island, informed us, quite suddenly, that he must return to them.

It is a walk to the beach, or beaches; there are several, all of them pebbly, and only one of them, Mazzaro, especially inhabited. The most attractive, Isola Bella, a guarded cove with water clear as barrel rain, is a mile and a half straight down; getting up again is the trick. A few times we have walked into Taormina and taken the bus, or a taxi. But mostly we go on foot. You can swim from March until Christmas (so the hearty souls say), but I confess I was not too enthusiastic until we bought the water mask. The mask had a round glass viewing plate, and a breathing tube that closes when you dive. Swimming silently among the rocks it is as though one had discovered a new visual dimension: in the underwater dusk a red phosphorescent fish looms at alarming proximity; your shadow drifts over a field of ermine-coloured grass; blue, silver bubbles rise from some long-legged sleeping thing lying in a field of blowing sea flowers . . .

If we do not go to the beach, then there is only one other reason for leaving the house: to shop in Taormina, and have an *apéritif* in the piazza. Taormina, really an extension of Naxos, the earliest Greek city in Sicily, has had a continuous existence from 396 B.C. Goethe explored here in 1787; he describes it thus: 'Now sitting at the spot where formerly sat the uppermost spectators, you confess at once that never did any audience, in any theatre, have before it such a spectacle as you there behold.'

From *The Dogs Bark: Public People and Private Places*,

TRUMAN CAPOTE

WATER

In the deep sea of Sicily, things go on changing and things go on staying the same. At the end of 1995 I came up for air, though like Cola Pesce I might've stayed underwater forever.

From *Midnight in Sicily*, PETER ROBB

Of the four elements water is the second least heavy and the second in respect of mobility. It is never at ease until it unites with its maritime element, where, when not disturbed by the winds, it establishes itself and remains with its surface equidistant from the centre of the world. It is the increase and humour of all vital bodies; without it nothing retains its first form. It unites and augments bodies by its increase.

Nothing lighter than itself can penetrate it without violence.

It readily raises itself by heat in thin vapour through the air. Cold causes it to freeze. Stagnation makes it foul. That is, heat sets it in movement, cold causes it to freeze, immobility corrupts it.

It assumes every odour, colour and flavour, and of itself it has nothing. It percolates through all porous bodies. Against its fury no human defence avails, or if it should avail it is not for long. In its rapid course it often serves as a support to things heavier than itself.

That power shows itself to be greater which is impressed upon a weaker, that is, a lesser resistance.

This conclusion is universal and it avails for the flow and ebb to prove that the sun or moon impresses itself so much the more upon the object, that is upon the waters, as they are of less depth; and therefore the shallow waters of the marshes must receive the cause of the ebb and flow with greater efficacy than do the mighty depths of the ocean.

From *The Notebooks of Leonardo da Vinci*

WATERMARK

It all felt like arriving in the provinces, in some unknown, insignificant spot – possibly one's own birthplace – after years of absence. In no small degree did this sensation owe to my own anonymity, to the incongruity of a lone figure on the steps of the *stazione*: an easy target for oblivion. Also, it was a winter night. And I remembered the opening line of one of Umberto Saba's poems that I'd translated long before, in a previous incarnation, into Russian: 'In the depths of the wild Adriatic . . .' In the depths, I thought, in the boondocks, in a lost corner of the wild Adriatic . . . Had I simply turned around, I'd have seen the *stazione* in all its rectangular splendor of neon and urbanity, seen block letters saying VENEZIA. Yet I didn't. The sky was full of winter stars, the way it often is in the provinces. At any point, it seemed, a dog could bark in the distance, or else you might hear a rooster. With my eyes shut I beheld a tuft of freezing seaweed splayed against a wet, perhaps ice-glazed, rock somewhere in the universe, oblivious to its location. I was that rock, and my left palm was that splayed tuft of seaweed. Presently a large, flat boat, something of a cross between a sardine can and a sandwich, emerged out of nowhere and with a thud nudged the *stazione*'s landing. A handful of people pushed ashore and raced past me up the stairs into the terminal. Then I saw the only person I knew in that city; the sight was fabulous.

There is something primordial about traveling on water, even for a short distance. You are informed that you are not supposed to be there not so much by your eyes, ears, nose, palate or palms as by your feet, which feel odd acting as an organ of sense. No matter how solid its substitute – the deck – under your feet, on water you are somewhat more alert than ashore, your faculties are more poised. On water, for instance, you never get absent-minded the way you do in the street; your legs keep you and your wits in constant check, as if you were some kind of compass. Well, perhaps what sharpens your wits while traveling on water is indeed a distant, roundabout echo of the good old chordates. At any rate, your sense of the other on water gets keener, as though heightened by a common as well as a mutual danger. The loss of direction is a psychological category as much as it is a navigational one. Be that as it may, for the next ten minutes, although we were moving in the same direction, I saw the arrow of the only person I knew in that city and mine diverge by at least 45 degrees. Most likely because this part of the Canal Grande was better lit.

JOSEPH BRODSKY

107

THE PALACE

The stones of Venice were green with slime. They were as dank and close as the cell I had just left. I arrived in the city only to spend my first days like a rat creeping along the edges of that network of grandiose sewers. My disguise was still new to me, it felt untested and I unsure. It seemed that at every turn of an alleyway someone would challenge me. Where the city echoed with its own mysterious orchestra of voices and water, for me it seemed to contain a constant threat of mocking laughter. Clothed in the fopperies I had bought and stolen along the way, I felt more naked than in my own skin.

Every fishwife and urchin, but mostly every soldier who passed me, turned me from a man into a cold-blooded animal, a reptile, a crawling thing, transfixed by fear to the dank stone. I was sure they could recognize my fine breeches for what they were, stolen from the corpse of a slain soldier in a ditch outside Forlì. And the hose and boots that I had been so pleased to find on his dead legs, surely they sighed out supernatural messages in the dark, signalling their origin. The concealed bloodstain on the toe of my right foot, that darkness calling out from the leather, did it not tell of desecration?

During my first weeks in that watery city, every time a priest passed me, nursing the hem of his dark robes over the oozing filth, I was ready to sink to my knees and confess to both my fraud and theft. But these priests were always hurrying. They took no interest in me and my raw soul. There was an outbreak of ague in the city. The rich were buried by day and the poor by night. It was said that there were scarcely enough hours to bury the dead and that the cemetery island of San Michele had coffins piled up on its shores.

. . . Under the sinister mists of Venice there was a layer of immunity. There were other layers, as many as in the strata of a rock, but at first I was too nervous to look at them. There was the olive-green water of the lagoon, the stone, the brick and the fog; beyond that I was afraid to go, not knowing what putrefying layers I would discover in between. Had it not been for my appointment with Vitelli, I would most certainly have fled.

How that city teased me! Inside and out, there was nothing but reflections. I was steered through the sluggish waters along with hundreds of other foreigners in the city.

How cold that city was: a great watery tomb submerged in its stinking finery. Venice had all the opalescent sheen of a fish's scales. The sickly winter sun shone through this bright transparency to the rotting flesh of the severed head inside. The sheen was a fake armour. Yet how proud they were of their sinking apparition! Before Giovanni entered my service, when words failed me, the subject of the miraculous beauty of the city saved me. The speech was fast and strange, a barbaric sing-song that lingered in my ear like licked-over whispers with slurred meanings. I learned to exchange a litany of praises. It seemed a lexicon of wonder had been handed down from generation to generation. Even the illiterate mud-pickers knew how to enumerate the treasures of St. Mark's. These things impressed me more than the fantasies of Carnival.

> *'O Venezia benedetta*
> *Non le vogio più lasar!'*

they sang, as they nursed their torn fishing nets and their lobster pots and their chilblains. I learned their refrains because I was like a parrot, repeating what I had heard with no notion of its meaning.

My affection for the place its inhabitants called the Empress of the Adriatic was feigned. It formed another rung on the ladder of lies that I climbed to become a gentleman. Yet, like so many of the other trappings, what began as a sham ended by being sincere. For, guided by Giovanni, my mathematical gondolier, I grew fond of that gloomy floating mausoleum. I grew to love the resonance of its empty halls, to look lovingly on the green nap of slime that coated the pediments of even the finest palaces. I grew to enjoy the false glitter and the prisms of cut crystal, the crocodile tears of blown Murano glass that dripped from every chandelier. Lulled by Giovanni's garrulous indolence, I became an admirer of Venice. I drifted along canals, steered by Giovanni Contarini. Giovanni, as was the custom, bore the name of the family his family had once worked for, which gave rise to endless stories of illegitimate daughters and sons of great noblemen in the city, together with whispered claims of their great fortunes.

I think the poorer citizens enjoyed the company of us outsiders. We were their captive audience. They had us prone in their funereal gondolas, adrift and at their mercy as they spilt out their secrets and their fantasies. It didn't matter whether one believed them or not, they enjoyed telling the tale; that was enough. Giovanni proved no exception: every journey we made, he contrived to pass by the pink and white wedding cake of the Ca' Contarini, the better to tell of his own claims.

LISA ST AUBIN DE TERÁN

Very dark under the great carob tree as we go down the steps. Dark still the garden. Scent of mimosa, and then of jasmine. The lovely mimosa tree invisible. Dark the stony path. The goat whinnies out of her shed. The broken Roman tomb which lolls right over the garden track does not fall on me as I slip under its massive tilt. Ah, dark garden, dark garden, with your olives and your wine, your medlars and mulberries and many almond trees, your steep terraces ledged high up above the sea, I am leaving you, slinking out. Out between the rosemary hedges, out of the tall gate, on to the cruel steep stony road. So under the dark, big eucalyptus trees, over the stream, and up toward the village. There, I have got so far.

Ah, the lovely morning! Away behind us the sun was just coming above the sea's horizon, and the sky was all golden, all a joyous fire-heated gold, and the sea was glassy bright, the wind gone still, the waves sunk into long, low undulations, the foam of the wake was pale ice-blue in the yellow sea. Sweet, sweet wide morning on the sea, with the sun coming, swimming up, and a tall sailing barque, with her flat fore-ladder sails delicately across the light, and a far-far steamer on the electric, vivid morning horizon.

The lovely dawn: the lovely pure, wide morning in the mid-sea, so golden-aired and delighted, with the sea-like sequins shaking, and the sky, far, far, far above, unfathomably clear. How glad to be on a ship! What a golden hour for the heart of man! Ah, if one could sail for ever, on a small, quiet, lonely ship, from land to land and isle to isle, and saunter through the spaces of this lovely world, always through the spaces of this lovely world. Sweet it would be sometimes to come to the opaque earth, to block oneself off against the stiff land, to annul the vibration of one's flight against the inertia of our terra firma! but life itself would be in the flight, the tremble of space.

From *Sea and Sardinia*, D.H. LAWRENCE

It is useless to look at Etruscan things for 'uplift'. If you want uplift, go to the Greek and the Gothic. If you want mass, go to the Roman. But if you love the odd spontaneous forms that are never to be standardized, go to the Etruscans. In the fascinating little Palazzo Vitelleschi one could spend many an hour, but for the fact that the very fullness of museums makes one rush through them.

From *Etruscan Places*, D.H. LAWRENCE

LA STORIA

Asked in 1972 if there were any archives that might explain why Sicilians left for America at the turn of the century, the mayor of Racalmuto answered, 'You want to know why people left? Hunger, that's why.' If one insisted on archives, he answered again, 'What archives? They fled here without regrets and most of them clandestinely. What records?' And he held up his fingers in a bunch as emphasis. 'They were dying of hunger.' Of course there was much truth in this. An old man who had left Sicily around 1898 recalled:

It was unbearable. My brother Luigi was six then and I was seven. Every morning we'd get up before sunrise and start walking about four or five miles to the farm of the *patrunu* – the boss. Many times we went without breakfast. For lunch we ate a piece of bread and plenty of water. If we were lucky, sometimes we would have a small piece of cheese or an onion. We worked in the hot sun until the late afternoon, then we had to drag ourselves home. We got there exhausted, just before sunset, so tired we could barely eat and fell asleep with all our clothes on. If we complained that the work was too hard our mother – God rest her soul – would say, 'And who is going to give you something to eat?' And life went on this way day in and day out, until *si vidiva surci virdi* – 'we began to see green mice.'

In the 1860s it was generally assumed that Italians by nature were 'as attached to their soil as an oyster to its rock.' Italians were not the only ones who clung to that belief. William Dean Howells, who became the first American consul to Venice in the 1860s, explained in *Venetian Life* (1866) that Italians were 'a home-loving people,' hardly the sort to abandon their native land for foreign shores. Throughout his travels in Italy he had not noted 'any perceptible movement of group emigration.' He was pleased to report that he had seen only one advertisement promoting emigration, a poster for a German steamship company in a small town bearing the unfortunate name of 'Colica'. After returning to America, Howells emerged as one of America's foremost novelists and social critics. By the time he died in 1920 at the age of eighty-three, more than 4.5 million Italians had entered the country.

An Italian statesman in 1870 cautioned that 'although we have made Italy, we have yet to make Italians.

Less than a decade after Italy had been 'unified', the emigration of Italians began accelerating at a phenomenal rate. During the next fifty years the exodus was to grow into one of the greatest migrations in world history, reducing Italy's population by one third.

A group of peasants in Lombardy, responding to an 1878 ministerial decree urging the population not to abandon the nation by emigrating, pointedly equated the definition of 'nation' with its ability to provide a decent livelihood for its people:

> What do you mean by a nation, Mr Minister? Is it the
> throng of the unhappy? Aye, then we are truly a nation . . .
> We plant and we reap wheat but never do we eat white
> bread. We cultivate the grape but we drink no wine. We
> raise animals for food but we eat no meat. We are clothed
> in rags . . . And in spite of all this, you counsel us, Mr
> Minister, not to abandon our country. But is that land,
> where one cannot live by one's toil, one's country?

In their search for a land where they could 'live by toil,' the emigrants at first restricted their travel to European countries. But soon, lured by the belief that Latin Argentina and Brazil would be more congenial for Italians, they braved the Atlantic to migrate to those countries. When a yellow fever epidemic in Brazil killed nine thousand Italians, the emigrants changed their primary destination to North America, mainly the United States, where cheap labor was greatly in demand. The Italians from the northern regions were the first to leave in large numbers. The southerners, more conservative – though with less reason – did not succumb to the lure of America until the late 1880s, but once they began to leave, they migrated in droves.

Northern Italy, center of the unification movement, implemented laws benefiting the areas north of Rome, leaving the South to stagnate while contributing taxes for northern economic expansion. The flow of northern emigrants diminished, while those from the South increased. At least four fifths of the arriving immigrants hailed from the seven regions south of Rome.

The American writer William Weyl, investigating emigration in the *Mezzogiorno*, found that the mass exodus had added another serious component to the 'Southern Problem': the moral and physical decay of communities in the aftermath of depopulation. 'The village is dead,' wrote Weyl in his commentary on ghost towns.

Nowhere is there the vibrant toil of young men; nowhere the cheerful sound of intense, hopeful activity. Its people, aimlessly filling a weird, fatal silence, seem like denizens of an accursed land. Their only thought is America. Periodically some new group receives prepaid tickets. A house is given up, and sold for nothing; a few listless farewells are made. For a moment the incurious village is galvanized into a vague sporadic interest. Then it lapses into its wonted lethargic state.

The late 1980s saw the greatest number of immigrants to the United States since World War II, but this time the smallest number were from Italy.

Much has been gained in economic well-being, in opportunities for greater possibilities, greater horizons. John Ciardi's father was a shoemaker, Joe DiMaggio's father was a fisherman, Mario Cuomo's parents were grocers.

Yet there is also a yearning for the home left behind – and more so for the second generation, whether it be the home of childhood or the land their parents left.

All immigrants, from the first English Puritans to the latest arrivals, have felt this yearning – a sense of loss (even guilt) and of anxiety at tearing up home roots. For this reason the word 'home' has a special meaning in America.

There is no word for 'home' in Italian. There is *casa* (house), *fucolaro* (hearth), but no word for home (as if they had no need for it) as in English.

JERRE MANGIONE & BEN MORREALE

LA FAMIGLIA

Among the many changes life in the New World brought, changes in the family affected the immigrant most deeply.

Nominally, the family was patriarchal. The father ruled the family as long as he remained in good health and was the chief breadwinner. In old age the eldest son superseded him, but even then the father retained much of his prestige. In some areas of the *Mezzogiorno* where traditions were more likely to be observed, the father's authority was considered absolute; no new dresses were purchased, no doctor consulted, no gifts made, no employment accepted without his approval.

Outwardly, at least, the father's decisions were accepted as law, even among his married children. To criticize one's father was considered sacrilege. Nonetheless, the typical Italian father frequently demonstrated affection for his children (though less frequently in public for his wife). He played with the youngest ones at home and took the older children on picnics in the country. But his insistence that they comply with his rules of conduct, which were sometimes enforced with corporal punishment, made the children regard their father with mixed feelings of fear and love.

If the husband lacked the qualities that made for benevolent despotism, it was often the wife who assumed command of the family while publicly wearing the mask of submissiveness. Under this guise she was able to take actions which traditionally were husbandly prerogatives. Such a wife would rarely contradict her husband in the presence of strangers, but once left alone with her eldest children, she would drop the mask of docile wife and 'speak her own mind openly and eloquently.'

The rules governing family life were simple and explicit, according to *la vie vecchia* (the old way):

1. Fear God and respect the saints or else you will really repent it.
2. The father is the father and he is experienced. The son will never fail if he imitates him.
3. The elders are prudent and experienced; do as they do and you will learn and prosper.
4. Always honor and obey your parents; then even the stones will love you.
5. If you don't listen to your helpful mother, everything will turn to shit right in your pants.
6. Father is the master.
7. Experience gives power.
8. Work hard, work always, and you will never know hunger.
9. Work honestly, and don't think of the rest.
10. Whoever doesn't want to work, dies like a dog.

Some of these rules were at the core of the conflicts that developed in immigrant families as the children became old enough to perceive the duality of their lives.

The Italian family gradually began to change. Women found freedom to play a larger role in and out of the family; sons refused to follow the work of the fathers, which brought about tensions and uncovered the not-so-loving Italian family so often seen in the stereotypes in such films as *The Godfather* and *Moonstruck*.

The concept of family with which immigrants came to America was as old as Italy itself. Sexuality was not mentioned, in spite of the fact that it was sex that attracted the man to the young girl who was walked in the *piazza* and to church by her mother for this very purpose. The woman came to marriage wor-shipped as a virgin and yet feared for her sexual powers. Sexuality became the complaint in the literature of the country for cen-turies. Dante condemned Francesca and Paolo to being *insiemi* ('joined') for eternity, Paolo wearily moaning and Francesca with a slight smile on her face. The complaint persisted to Lampedusa, whose Prince in *The Leopard* lamented, '. . . how can I find satis-faction with a woman who makes the sign of the cross in bed before every embrace and then at the crucial moment just cries "Gesumaria!" When we married and she was sixteen I found that rather exciting; but now . . . seven children I've had with her, seven; and never once have I seen her navel . . . Is that right?'

If this was the mentality of a prince in the nineteenth cen-tury, Corrado Niscemi could speak of it from another angle in 1968: 'Sex is without love in this country; it is an act of rage and bitterness, not tenderness. The man pins the woman to the bed with the attitude "I work hard to support you; the least you can do is to give me a male child."'

Although marriage produced relationships which created a public image of unity and warmth, privately they often seethed with tension. In the New World such tensions were intensified. The husband came with the tradition of *gallismo* (roosterism) on his side, the wife with the Church as an ally and the confessional a center of conspiracy. Men, in turn, regarded the Church as an enemy and secretly looked upon Christ as a prime *cornutu* (cuck-old) for letting himself be killed in the manner of a common criminal. The men's curse words are evidence to that effect.

Many Italian proverbs demonstrate male attitudes towards women:

Like a good weapon, she should be cared for properly.

Like a hat, she should be kept straight.

Like a mule, she should be given plenty of work and occasional beatings.

Above all, a woman should be kept in her place as subordinate.

Life for those peasant women was not easy. In Italy they had been governed by the Napoleonic Code, which gave women few rights and many responsibilities. Certainly, they had the concern for the family. They had to fetch water from the well, wash the family clothes in a public water trough, bake bread, prepare food, shop and bargain, and, weather and time permitting, roam the open fields with their children for dandelions or wild fennel. In the fall they gathered *ristucia* (twigs and dried wheat stalks) and returned with a giant bundle on their head, children beside them. They helped harvest olives, almonds, and walnuts, and hired themselves out to gather grapes for the making of wine. Women were also *levatrici* – midwives (doctor, pharmacist all in one), who did cupping, set leeches, brought infants into the world, and helped bury the dead.

From *The Italian Americans: Troubled Roots*, ANDREW ROLLE

ON VENETIAN WOMEN

The women of Venice are very handsome, and very vain. They are tall, they walk beautifully, and they are often fair (in the sixteenth century Venetian ladies used to bleach their hair in the sunshine, training it through crownless hats like vines through a trellis). Their eyes are sometimes a heavy-lidded greenish-blue, like the eyes of rather despondent armadillos. Rare indeed is a dishevelled Venetian woman, and even the Madonnas and female saints of the old masters are usually elegantly dressed. The most slovenly people to be seen in the city are nearly always tourists – cranks and water-colour artists apart.

The Venetians are not, by and large, rich: but they have always spent a large proportion of their money on clothes and ornaments and you will hardly ever see a girl dressed for pottering, in a sloppy sweater and a patched skirt, or in that unpressed deshabille that marks the utter emancipation of the Englishwoman. The girls at the University, who are either studying languages, or learning about Economics and Industrial Practices, look more like models than academics; and the housemaids, when they walk off in scented couples for their weekend pleasures, would hardly seem out of place at Ascot, or at a gala convention of the Women Lawyers' Association.

This love of dress is deep-rooted in the Venetian nature. The men are very dapper, too, and until quite recently used to cool themselves with little fans and parasols in the Public Gardens – 'curious', as Augustus Hare observed austerely in 1896, 'to English eyes'. As early as 1299 the Republic introduced laws restricting ostentation, and later the famous sumptuary laws were decreed, strictly governing what people might wear, with a special magistracy to enforce them. They were never a success. When the Patriarch of Venice forbade the use of 'excessive ornaments', a group of women appealed directly to the Pope, who promptly restored them their jewellery. When the Republic prohibited long gowns, the Venetian women caught up their trains in intricate and delicious folds, fastened with sumptuous clasps. When it was announced that only a single row of pearls might be worn, with a maximum value of 200 ducats, the evasions of the law were so universal, so ingenious and so brazen that the magistracy gave up and turned its disapproving eyes elsewhere. In the eighteenth century Venetian women were the most richly dressed in Europe, and it took an Englishwoman, Lady Mary Wortley Montagu, to observe that 'since everybody wore masks at the opera anyway, there was consequently no trouble in dressing'. Among the patrician ladies of old Venice, as among the women of Arabian harems, there was nothing much to think about but clothes and babies. Venetian *mores* were bred out of Byzantium, and respectable women were closely guarded and carefully circumscribed. Clamped in their houses out of harm's way, they were little more than tools or playthings, western odalisques; even the Doge's wife had no official position. No item of dress was more popular among Venetian aristocrats than the absurd towering clogs, sometimes twenty inches high, which obliged their wives to totter about with the help of two servants (and which, since they made great height socially desirable, have perhaps left a legacy in the unshakeable determination of modern Venetian women to wear the highest possible heels in all circumstances).

Only two women have played parts of any prominence in Venetian history. The first was Caterina Cornaro, who married the King of Cyprus in 1472 and was officially adopted as a 'daughter of the Republic' in order to ensure Venetian control of the island. Her husband died a year after their marriage, the Venetians took over, and poor Caterina languished away in gilded exile at Asolo, signing herself to the last as 'Queen of Cyprus, Jerusalem and Armenia, Lady of Asolo'. The second was Bianca Cappello, daughter of a noble house, who ran away with a Florentine clerk in 1564. She was condemned to death *in absentia*, such was the disgrace of it all, but presently rose in the world to become Grand Duchess of Tuscany, and was promptly re-clasped to the Venetian bosom as another 'daughter of the Republic'. She died of poisoning in 1587, but the Republic did not go into mourning, just in case it was the Grand Duke who had poisoned her.

It was only in the eighteenth century that the upper class Venetian woman came into her own, and even now a cloistered feeling of anachronism often surrounds her. Sometimes a beautiful young blonde is to be seen in Venice, gracefully rowing her own boat, but the gondoliers do not even consider the possibility that she might be Venetian, and airily point her out as English, American or German, according to the nationality of their passengers. With her maids, her always exquisite clothes, her waiting gondolier, and the almost insuperable difficulty she has of getting out of one cushioned gondola and into another, the Venetian lady is scarcely the kind to go messing about in boats. She is often rich and often influential ('the flat downstairs,' I was once informed by a house agent, 'is occupied by a lady, with her husband') but there are few professional women in the city, and one sometimes pines, in an ambience so perfumed and cossetted, for a hard-boiled New York career girl, with her heart – or part of it, anyway – deep in the propagation of soap flakes.

Other classes of Venetian women were not so sheltered under the Republic. Burghers' wives and daughters were always freer and often better educated. Poor women lived a life of rugged equality and Venetian working women today are often jolly, gregarious characters, like figures from a Goldoni comedy, throwing hilarious ribaldries across the post-office counter, or sitting plumply at their knitting on the quayside. Courtesans in sixteenth century Venice were not only celebrated and honoured, but often people of cultivation, with a taste for art and poetry (though the law at one time decreed that each such girl must carry a red light at the prow of her gondola). In earlier centuries there was a celebrated brothel, the Casteletto, at the end of the Rialto bridge, famous throughout Europe for the beauty and skill of its girls. Later, when Venice was beginning her decline, the prostitutes became courtesans, increased in wealth and respectability, burst the confines of the bordels, and gave the city its lasting reputation for lascivious charm. At the end of the sixteenth century there are said to have been 2,889 patrician ladies in Venice, and 2,508 nuns, and 1,936 burgher women: but there were 11,654 courtesans, of whom 210 were carefully registered in a catalogue by a public-spirited citizen of the day, together with their addresses and prices – or, as the compiler delicately put it, 'the amount of money to be paid by noblemen and others desirous of entering their good graces.' The cheapest charged one *scudo*, the most expensive thirty, and the catalogue reckons that the enjoyment of them all would cost the intemperate visitor 1,200 gold *scudi*.

A scholarly Venetian once remarked that his city had fostered three bad practices hitherto unknown in Italy – adulation, Lutheranism and debauchery: but he did not sound altogether censorious. Venice in her heyday, despite a streak of salty puritanism in her character, was tolerant about sex. A favourite subject of the Venetian masters, it has been observed, was Christ Defending the Woman Taken in Adultery, and even the established church was fairly easy-going with libertines: it was only with reluctance and after long delay that the administration of the Basilica, in the seventeenth century, closed the chapel of San Clemente because of the scandalous things that were known to go on behind the altar. Gay young nuns were seen on visiting days in habits distinctly *décolletés*, and with clusters of pearls in their virginal hair. In the wildest days of carnival even the Papal Nuncio used to wear a domino. Family chaplains looked benignly upon the Venetian institution of the *cicisbeo*, the handsome young man who, in the dying years of the Republic, used to stand in constant attendance upon each great lady of Venice, even sometimes helping her maids to dress her. 'The only honest woman in Venice', a wry husband remarked to a friend one day, 'is that one there' – and he pointed to a little stone figure carved on a wall above a bridge. Venice took his point, and to this day the bridge, near the Frari church, is called The Bridge of the Honest Woman.

JAN MORRIS

STREETS FULL OF WATER

The life-steam of Venice arrives on wheels – her goods and her visitors, even the poor cattle for her municipal slaughter-house – but once at the station or the Piazzale Roma, all this mass of men and material, this daily army, must proceed by water or by foot. Thomas Coryat, before he visited Venice, met an English braggart who claimed to have 'ridden through Venice in post.' This was, as Coryat indignantly discovered, 'as gross and palpable a fiction as ever was coyned.' Nobody ever rode through Venice in post, and there are still no proper roads in the city, only footpaths and canals. '*Streets Full of Water*', Robert Benchley cabled home when he first arrived there, '*Please Advise*'.

JAN MORRIS

> *History scrapes the bottom*
> *like a drag net*
> *with a few rips and more than one fish escapes.*
> *Sometimes you meet the ectoplasm*
> *of an escapee and he doesn't seem particularly happy.*
> *He doesn't know he's outside, nobody told him.*
> *The others, in the bag, think*
> *they're freer than him.*

Satura, EUGENIO MONTALE

I *MALAVOGLIA*

After midnight the wind began to raise merry hell, as if all the cats in the village were on the roof, shaking the shutters. You could hear the sea lowing around the tall rocks so that it seemed as if the cattle from the Sant' Alfio market were gathered there, and day broke as black as a traitor's soul. A bad September

Sunday, in short, that sort of treacherous September day which suddenly throws up a storm, like a rifle shot among the prickly pears. The village boats were drawn up on the beach, and well moored to the boulders below the wash-place; and the local children were amusing themselves shouting and whistling whenever they saw the odd tattered sail pass by in the distance, in all that wind and mist, as though they were being driven along by the devil himself; but the women crossed themselves, as if they could clearly see the poor folk who were in those boats.

Maruzza la Longa said nothing, as was only right, but she couldn't be still for a moment, and kept going hither and thither through the house and the courtyard, like a hen when it is about to lay an egg. The men were at the wine shop, or in Pizzuto's barber's shop, or under the butcher's awning, pensively watching it pour down. The only people on the beach were padron 'Ntoni, because of that load of lupins he had at sea, along with the *Provvidenza* and his son Bastianazzo to boot, and la Locca's son, though he had nothing to lose, and all he had in the boat with the lupins was his brother Menico. Padron Fortunato Cipolla, while he was being shaved in Pizzuto's barber's shop, said that he didn't give two brass farthings for Bastianazzo and the load of lupins.

'Now they all want to play the dealer and get rich quick,' he said, shrugging; 'and they try to shut the stable door after the horse has gone.'

There was a crowd in Santuzza's wine shop: there was that drunkard Rocco Spatu, who was bawling and spitting fit for ten, compare Tino Piedipapera, mastro Turi Zuppiddo, compare Mangiacarrubbe, don Michele the customs man, with his trousers tucked into his boots and his pistol slung across his stomach, as though he were likely to go looking for smugglers in that weather, and compare Mariano Cinghialenta. That mammoth mastro Turi was jokingly dealing his friends punches that would have brought an ox to its knees, as though he still had his caulker's mallet in his hands, and then compare Cinghialenta started shouting and swearing, to show that he was a true red-blooded carter.

Zio Santoro, crouched under that bit of shelter, in front of the doorway, waited with his outstretched hand for someone to pass, so that he could ask for alms.

'Between the two of them, father and daughter,' said compare Turi Zuppiddo, 'they must be making a fine living, on a day like this, when so many people come to the wine shop.'

'Bastianazzo Malavoglia is worse off than he is, at this moment,' replied Piedipapera, 'and mastro Cirino can ring the bell for mass as hard as he pleases, the Malavoglia won't be going to church to-day; they're turning their backs on God, because of that cargo of lupins they've got at sea.'

The wind sent skirts and dry leaves swirling, so that Vanni Pizzuto, razor poised, would hold whoever he was shaving casually by the nose, to turn to look at the passers-by, and put his hand on his hips, with his hair all curly and shiny as silk; and the chemist stood at the door of his shop, wearing that awful great hat which gave the impression of acting as an umbrella, and pretending to have a serious discussion with don Silvestro the town clerk, so that his wife couldn't order him into church by force; and he snickered at this ruse, winking at the girls who were tripping along through the puddles.

'To-day,' Piedipapera was saying, 'padron 'Ntoni wants to play the heathen, like don Franco the chemist.'

'If you so much as turn your head to look at that impudent don Silvestro, I'll give you a slap right here where we stand,' muttered la Zuppidda to her daughter, as they were crossing the square. 'I don't like that man.'

At the last toll of the bell, Santuzza had put the wine shop into her father's care and gone into church, bringing the customers behind her. Zio Santoro, poor man, was blind, and it was no sin for him not to go to mass; that way no time was wasted in the wine shop, and he could keep an eye on the counter from the doorway, even though he couldn't see, because he knew the customers one by one just by their footsteps, when they came to drink a glass of wine.

'Santuzza's stockings,' observed Piedipapera, as Santuzza was picking her way past on tiptoe, dainty as a kitten, 'come rain or shine, Santuzza's stockings have been seen only by massaro Filippo the greengrocer; and that's the truth.'

'There are little devils abroad to-day,' said Santuzza, crossing herself with holy water. 'It's enough to drive you to sin.'

Nearby, la Zuppidda was gabbling Hail Maries, squatting on her heels and darting poisonous glances hither and thither as though she were in a fury with the whole village, and telling anyone who would listen: 'Comare la Longa isn't coming to church, even though her husband is at sea in this storm! Small wonder the good Lord is punishing us!' Menico's mother was there too, even though all she was good for was watching the flies go by!

'We should pray for sinners as well,' said Santuzza. 'That's what pure souls are for.'

'Yes, like the Mangiacarrubbe girl is doing, all pious behind her shawl, and goodness knows what vile sins she causes young men to commit.'

Santuzza shook her head, and said that when you're in church you shouldn't speak ill of your neighbour. 'The host has to smile at all comers,' replied la Zuppidda, and then, in la Vespa's ear: 'Santuzza is concerned that people are saying that she sells water for wine; but she would do better to think about not causing Filippo the greengrocer to commit a mortal sin, because he has a wife and children.'

'Myself,' replied la Vespa, 'I've told don Giammaria that I don't want to carry on in the Daughters of Mary, if they keep Santuzza on as leader.'

'Does that mean you've found a husband?' asked la Zuppidda.

'I have not found a husband,' snapped back la Vespa waspishly. 'I'm not one of those women who brings a string of men after them right into church, with polished shoes, or big paunches.'

The one with the paunch was Brasi, padron Cipolla's son, who was the darling of mothers and daughters alike, because he owned vines and olive groves.

'Go and see if the boat is properly moored,' his father said to him, making the sign of the cross.

No one could help thinking that the wind and rain were pure gold for the Cipolla family; that is how things go in this world, and once reassured that their boat was well-moored, they were rubbing their hands in glee at the storm; while the Malavoglia had turned quite white and were tearing their hair, because of that cargo of lupins they had bought on credit from zio Crocifisso Dumb bell.

'Shall we face facts?' snapped la Vespa. 'The really unlucky man is zio Crocifisso, who sold the lupins on credit.'

'If you give credit without a pledge, you'll lose your friend, the goods and the edge.'

Zio Crocifisso was kneeling at the foot of the altar of Our Lady of Sorrows, with plenty of beads to hand, and intoning the little verses in a nasal whine which would have melted the heart of Satan himself. Between Hail Maries there was talk of the lupin deal, and the *Provvidenza* which was on the high seas, and la Longa who had five children to look after.

'In this day and age,' said padron Cipolla, shrugging, 'nobody is content with their lot, and everybody wants to take heaven by storm.'

'The fact is,' concluded compare Zuppiddo, 'that this is a bad day for the Malavoglia.'

'Myself,' added Piedipapera, 'I wouldn't like to be in compare Bastianazzo's shoes.'

Dusk fell cold and gloomy; occasionally there was a gust of north wind, which brought down a little burst of fine, silent rain; it was one of those evenings when, if your boat was in harbour with its belly in the dry sand, you could enjoy seeing the pot steaming in front of you, with your child between your knees, listening to the woman padding about the house behind you. Layabouts preferred to spend that Sunday in the wine shop, and it looked as if Sunday was going to run into Monday, too, in the wine shop, and even the doorposts were warmed by the flames from the fire, so much so that zio Santoro, posted out there with his hand outstretched and chin on his knees, had drawn in a bit, to warm his old back up a little.

'He's better off than compare Bastianazzo, at this moment,' repeated Rocco Spatu, lighting his pipe at the door.

And without any more ado he put his hand into his pocket, and splashed out to the tune of two *centesimos* of alms.

'You're wasting your money thanking God you're safe at home,' Piedipapera told him. 'There's small danger that you'll end up like Bastianazzo.'

Everyone showed their appreciation of this sally, and then they looked from the doorway down to the sea, as black as the *sciara*, without saying another word.

Padron 'Ntoni had wandered around aimlessly all day, as though he had St Vitus' dance, and the chemist asked him if he were taking an iron cure, or just going for an idle stroll in that bad weather. 'Some providence, eh, padron 'Ntoni?' But the chemist was godless, everyone knew that.

La Locca's son was outside there with his hands in his pockets because he hadn't got a penny to his name, and he said:

'Zio Crocifisso has gone to look for padron 'Ntoni with Piedipapera, to get him to say that he bought the lupins on credit in front of witnesses.'

'That means he thinks they're in danger, along with the *Provvidenza*.'

'My brother Menico is with compare Bastianazzo on the *Provvidenza* too.'

'Well done – what we were saying was that if your brother doesn't come back, you will be head of the household.'

'He went because zio Crocifisso would only pay him half wages too, when he sent him out with the fishing boat, whereas the Malavoglia are paying him in full.' And when the others sniggered, he just stood slack-jawed.

At dusk Maruzza had gone to wait on the *sciara* with her younger children, because you could see quite a large stretch of sea from there, and she shuddered and scratched her head without a word when she heard it roar like that. The baby was crying and the poor creatures looked like lost souls, all alone on the *sciara*, at that hour. The baby's crying gave her a pang, poor woman, it struck her as a bad omen; and she couldn't think what to come up with to quieten her, and sang her little songs in an unsteady voice which had a quiver of tears about it too.

On their way from the wine shop with their oil pitchers or wine flasks, the neighbours stopped to have a word with la Longa as though nothing were wrong, and the odd friend of her husband Bastianazzo, compare Cipolla, for instance, or compare Mangiacarrubbe, coming over to the *sciara* to take a look at the sea and find out what sort of mood the old moaner was falling asleep in, asked la Longa about her husband, and stayed with her a bit to keep her company; smoking their pipes in silence right under her nose, or talking among themselves in low voices. Frightened by these unaccustomed attentions, the poor creature gazed at them in distress and clutched her child to her, as though they wanted to steal it away. At last the toughest or most compassionate of them took her by the arm and led her home. She let herself be led, calling desperately upon the holy Virgin in a vain attempt at consolation. Her children followed her, clinging to her skirts as though they were afraid that something might be stolen from them too. As they passed in front of the wine shop, all the customers came to the door amidst all the smoke, and fell silent as they watched her go by, as though she were already a curiosity.

'Requiem aeternam,' zio Santoro mumbled under his breath, 'that poor Bastianazzo always gave me charity when padron 'Ntoni left him a penny in his pocket.'

The poor creature still didn't realise that she was a widow, and kept calling stumblingly upon the Virgin to succour her.

A group of neighbourhood women were waiting for her in front of her balcony, chatting in low voices amongst themselves. When they saw her appear at the end of the street, comare Piedipapera and cousin Anna went towards her, their hands folded, without saying a word. Then she dug her nails into her hair with a desperate cry and ran to hide away in the house.

'What a disaster,' they were all saying on the street. 'Boat, cargo and all. More than forty *onze* of lupins!'

GIOVANNI VERGA

A History of
Contemporary Italy

The debrief report of one British officer makes interesting reading on popular attitudes:

> The feelings and support of the civilian population vary greatly. In the towns the great majority of the population are only concerned about their own skins. Many inveigh

against the Germans and some against the Partisans, but this is only because the Germans and Partisans are a cause of danger to their well-being and possibly to their lives. In the industrial towns there is, of course, a large Communist element, such as in Turin and Milan and they are all pro-Partisan. Then there are, of course, a few Fascists. The non-Partisan country areas are half-way between the two extremes of stupid, short-sighted selfishness and open support. The Partisan areas are almost entirely pro-Partisan with very few exceptions and the exceptions are generally very careful to hide their feelings. Generally speaking, the poorer the people are, the stronger is their support. This 'class-scale' applies on the whole to the entire country. The richest men in my area, which was a very poor one, were the least helpful to the Partisan cause – in fact, they did the least they could without getting into trouble. First, because being the richest men, they had been connected with the Fascist administration and, secondly, because, being rich, they wanted to be quite sure that neither Germans nor Partisans would cause them to lose their fortunes.

In my area the population were first-class. They were only too willing to give us a bed to sleep in and whatever food they had. I generally had my meals with some peasants who had their house and all their belongings burnt by the Germans, all their food reserves too. They lived in a barn where they previously kept their sheep, sleeping in their clothes on the straw. They had practically no blankets or change of clothing. They lost most of their cash, as when the Germans arrived they had but little warning and had to flee for their lives without having time to save their belongings. All they had left were a couple of barns, their land, a cow, and the clothes they stood in. They knew that what they had lost was due to their having identified themselves so openly with the Partisans and with British officers and yet never did they utter a word of complaint or reproach. They were always willing to give us food; in fact were most hurt when occasionally we ate elsewhere, and the same applied to any Partisan friend of theirs who happened to pass by. Naturally, we did all we could for them, such as giving them a parachute on the rare occasions when we had a drop. When the Germans came in their last *rastrellamento* prior to my departure on October 8th/10th, every civilian fled, of course, but the old lady who befriended us remained in her barn. 'If the Germans come here, they might kill me, but if I'm not here they are sure to burn my barn, and, in that case, it's just as well to die now,' she said. Luckily the Germans did not go there.

Most of the villages considered it an honour if any of us, officers or O/Rs, invited ourselves to a meal. Yet they knew what the penalty for helping either escaped POWs or Partisans was. All the streets of non-Partisan towns and villages are plastered with notices of the dreadful consequences which will be the lot of anybody assisting Partisans and POWs. Hundreds of British POWs have now regained their freedom or are still at large owing to the hospitality they received from peasants and country people,

hospitality given at very great risk to themselves. Many
have been guests (not paying guests) of families for over a
year, and they were complete strangers. There are many
just accusations which can be levelled at the Italian people
but their behaviour to escaped British POWs must not be
forgotten.

The Italian Resistance, if one does not count last-minute adher-
ents, probably numbered some 100,000 active members, and
many thousands of others who helped in some way. Of these,
35,000 died, 21,000 were mutilated and 9,000 were deported
to Germany – casualty figures far higher than those incurred in
regular warfare. After the war the British Hewitt Report came to
the conclusion that 'without these partisan victories there would
have been no Allied victory in Italy so swift, so overwhelming or
so inexpensive.'

The cost in human suffering had been very high. The refusal
to adopt the policy of *attendismo* or to limit the Resistance to
minor acts of sabotage had meant incurring the full brunt of
repression and German reprisals, of which the massacre of the
Ardeatine caves and the extermination of the villages of
Marzabotto were only the two most terrible examples. At the
end of Eric Newby's *Love and War in the Apennines* (based, as
with [Stuart] Hood's book, on his experiences as an escaped
prisoner of war), the peasant Francesco says, 'We've seen some
things here, my friends, we and our children. Let's hope that it
will never be like that again.'

The sacrifices of the Resistance were not made in vain. At a
time when the Italians were very widely despised and discredited

for their acceptance and support of Mussolini's regime, the Partisans did much to salvage Italy's tarnished image and give the Italians new faith in themselves. Furthermore, they succeeded in creating a lasting tradition of anti-Fascism.

PAUL GINSBORG

LOVE AND WAR IN THE APENNINES

To all those Italians who helped me,
and thousands like me, at the risk of their lives,
I dedicate this book.

We were captured off the east coast of Sicily on the morning of the twelfth of August, 1942, about four miles out in the Bay of Catania. It was a beautiful morning. As the sun rose I could see Etna, a truncated cone with a plume of smoke over it like the quill of a pen stuck in a pewter inkpot, rising out of the haze to the north of where I was treading water.

About eight o'clock we were picked up by some Sicilian fishermen who hauled us into their boat like a lot of half-dead fish. They were surprised. We were thankful, although we knew that we would now never make the rendezvous off Capo Campolato which had been fixed for the following night if we failed to reach the submarine by one o'clock in the morning of the twelfth.

[Then later, further north, Newby's taken into hiding.]

Down by the riverside.

When I woke and pulled the pack off my head it was already light, but there was a dense fog and it was very quiet. It was like being wrapped in cotton wool. The frogs had stopped croaking and the mosquitoes had gone. The air was cold but I was glad that it was. After having slept with my head in the pack I had a splitting headache and a horrible mouth; otherwise, apart from one or two giant mosquito bites on my neck, I was unscathed.

I stayed in my sleeping-bag until the fog began to turn yellow in the light of the rising sun. Then I got up, cleaned my teeth, rolled up the sleeping-bag, which was very wet, put on my left boot and set off through the wood, parallel to the track, in what I imagined must be the direction of the river. My other foot was a soggy amalgam of mud and plaster, but I no longer cared. It didn't hurt anymore. The rough treatment which it had received ever since I had injured it, seemed to have done it good.

After about twenty minutes I emerged on the edge of a dried-out backwater of a river. The banks were loose shingle and the bottom was filled with big, round stones which I found difficult to cross. The far bank was covered with a dense growth of what looked to me like dwarf acacia trees, in which I lost myself in a maze of sheep runs which led nowhere. It was a creepy place full of dung, but after blundering about in it for a bit I suddenly came out on the right bank of the river.

It was a marvellous, unforgettable sight, especially for some-one like myself who had seen nothing for a year except walls, barbed wire and, at the best, a rather humdrum domestic coun-try. I was on an inside curve of a big bend in the river. Here it was about 250 yards wide. Although it was low, it was running strongly. The water was the colour of milky coffee, and in places it erupted and formed whirlpools which whirled for a time before they collapsed, and on its surface there were gouts of foam, like clotted cream which the current seized and swept away. The fog was going now, rolling away upstream to the west in a series of giant billows, all golden in the sun. Downstream was the dried-out channel I had just crossed, with a deep pool in a sort of bay at the mouth of it, from which a long spur of stone embankment curved away. It was unfin-ished, and on top of it there were piles of fascines that looked like sausage rolls filled with stones, and the remains of the work-men's fires, although no work seemed to have been done on the embankment for some time. Behind it there was a plantation of willows in which the saplings had been cut down to make the fascines.

Soon the sun was hot and I decided to swim. It was a crazy thing to do, but there was no one about. I crossed over to the pool at the mouth of the backwater, took off my clothes and plunged in. It was icy. Perhaps it seemed colder than it was because I was rather thin. Then I dressed, ate some food from my pack and hobbled back to the wood.

The plaster of paris was like a great lump of chewed nougat, and I cut it off, using the knife that the *maestro* had given me. Then I lay down under the trees to wait for Giovanni.

It was deliciously cool there. The sun beat down on the tops of the poplars, but they were so close together that it only succeeded here and there in sending down long shafts of dappled light into the green, damp shadow of the wood. Their slender trunks soared upwards like columns and the intervals between them were dim, green aisles. It was like being in a cathedral that had been engulfed by the sea. Then I fell asleep.

*

I was awakened by someone tugging at my arm. Standing over me there was a man with a big brown moustache, and with a thick head of hair which was just beginning to go grey over the ears.

'You sleep too strongly,' he said. 'I have been waiting for ten minutes and I am tired of it. I am called Giovanni. I have brought you a picnic,' he said. He called it *una merenda*. 'We shall eat it by the river. Then later we shall go to my house.'

He was dressed in an old suit of snuff-coloured velveteen and over his shoulder he had a sack which presumably contained the *merenda*. He was a powerful-looking man, about five feet eight but with a chest like a barrel and a long scar down one side of his nose. He walked with a limp. We went back towards the river, more or less by the route which I had followed before. My ankle now hurt abominably, but at least it stood up to being used just as well without the plaster.

Eventually we reached the bank of the dry backwater that I had already crossed, but farther upstream. Here, beyond the shadow of the trees, the light was incandescent: the stones so hot that I felt they might explode. On the far side there was a path leading through the dwarf trees, and after following it for a bit we came out in a small clearing behind the hut I had seen earlier which stood high above the embankment on a little forest of piles.

'My house in the country,' Giovanni said. He went up a ladder to it and unlocked the door. Inside there was a room about eight feet square with a bunk on one side, some cooking pots, a fishing rod, a pair of decayed rubber waders, and that was about all.

L'è'ura d'mangar – 'Time to eat' – he said. He spoke the dialect which here, on the river bank, sounded even deeper and more mysterious than it had at the farm on the first night that I was free. I told him I couldn't understand it and he said that, in future, he would speak Italian, and very slowly.

We sat outside in the shade and ate a delicious meal, the best of its kind that I could remember. Everything was homemade.

E nostrano, he said, whenever he offered me anything. No wonder he had brought a sack. We ate a delicious, thick soup full of vegetables and *pasta* that was made in the shape of sea shells which he ladled from a pot; and we ate *polenta*, a sort of solidified yellow porridge made from maize, which he sliced with a piece of wire; wonderful hard white bread, made from something called *pasta dura* and with it slices of *culatello*, a kind of unsmoked ham from part of the pig's behind that was cut so thinly that it was almost transparent which, he said, was a local speciality; and there was another sort called *spalla*, made from the shoulder, which he said was the sort that Verdi preferred, but I thought the *culatello* was the best.

'It's good, the *culatello*,' he said, relapsing into the dialect and offering me more.

We drank Lambrusco from a black bottle which held two

litres. The cork was similar to a champagne cork but without the metal cap with the maker's name on it, and it was prevented from blowing out of the mouth of the bottle by strong thread which was lashed down over the top of it and round the lip. The Italian word for cork was *turacciolo* but he called it *bouchon* in the dialect which seemed to have a lot of French words in it. The wine was deep purple and it seethed in the glasses with its own natural gas. The same wine the farmer had given me on that first night. And then we ate cheese that had been maturing for two years in one of his barns.

Afterwards, we lay on our stomachs on the grass on the slope of the embankment, looking out over the top of it across the river, and he told me about his life. It took a long time because he found Italian difficult.

Before the war he had been one of the men employed on the river in rowing boats to shift the leading marks and buoys for the barges which went up to Mantova, which had to be done constantly because the bed of the stream was always changing. It was a hard way of earning a living which he had combined with that of being a fisherman. His wife had died in childbirth in 1937. Until six months ago he had been in the navy with some special force, rather like the one I had been captured with, training on a lonely part of the west coast, when somebody had dropped a snatch block on his foot and he had been invalided out. Now he lived with his mother and with his father, who had been both fisherman and farmer, in a house near the dyke. He was anti-German, anti-Mussolini, anti-King and anti-Badoglio who, he considered, had betrayed Italy and then left it in the soup.

'From now on I'm Communist,' he said. I would have liked to have talked to him more about this, but that was all he would say and I was really content to leave it at that. The war seemed far away. It might never have happened. Looking out on this dreamlike landscape it was difficult to believe that a few miles away *feldgendarmen* and *carabinieri* were after one's blood. And they might even be closer.

Occasionally, far off, I could hear a train rumbling across some bridge, whistling mournfully. Otherwise, there were no sounds, not even the barking of a dog to disturb the silence of that long, golden afternoon, during which I sometimes dozed and sometimes listened to Giovanni as he droned on, with lots of careful explanation, about his beloved river.

Even when it was in normal flood in October or November, the wood in which I had slept would be deep under water, and from the main dyke beyond it to the one on the other bank where it ran away from the salient where the village was, at least three kilometres would be like an inland sea.

'That's the time when I take down my little hut,' he said, 'otherwise it would end up in the Adriatic.'

In winter it was bitterly cold here and there were terrible fogs – there was fog about seventy days a year – which obliterated everything. Down near the mouth of the river, in the delta, were the *valli*, vast enclosures of brackish water, separated by dykes. In winter these shallows were invaded by clouds of migrant ducks and wild geese and men like Giovanni, who was mad for shooting, waited, shivering, for the flights at dawn and dusk, or else stalked them, using punts. The *valli* were also the hunting grounds of men called *fiocinini*, fish poachers, who took eels by night from under the noses of the keepers of the *valli*. On dark, stormy nights in November millions of eels were on the move in the river valley, all travelling eastwards on the first stage of their journey to the Sargasso Sea where, in the depths of the Atlantic, they would beget their young; a journey from which only the new-born eels returned.

'No one knows what happens to those that make the journey,' Giovanni said, 'but some don't go at all and they become as fat as eunuchs.'

Of those that did make the journey, thousands and thousands were caught in the great eel traps at Comacchio in the *valli*. Once thirty-four tons of eels were taken there in a single night, and to celebrate the catch a mortar was fired and wine distributed. And he spoke about the other fish that inhabited the river; carp, fish called *cavadane* and *pescegatto*, and the big sturgeon that sometimes came up it. Finally, aroused by so much talk of fish, he showed me how the big net worked which I had seen from further downstream that morning, which was what he called a *bilancione* because it was operated by counter-balancing weights. He let fly some tackle and the net lowered itself into the water like a giant, prehistoric bird fishing and then, when he hauled on a rope, it rose again.

By this time the sun was setting. The air was becoming chilly and there was a mistiness in the woods far off up and down stream.

Anduma a cà, said Giovanni. 'Let's go home.' He threw the remains of the picnic, which was not much, into the river, put the pot which had contained the soup back into his sack, locked up his hut and set off through the trees. It was one of the best days I could remember, and I hated the thought that it was almost at an end.

ERIC NEWBY

IF NOT NOW, WHEN?

Chaim said, 'Let's not behave like enemies: we're not enemies. Come down from the car, let's sit on the grass. They've detached the locomotive; your train won't leave for at least two hours. You see: there's something important to discuss.' They all got out of the train and sat in a circle on the grass, in the resin-scented air, under a sky swept clean by a high wind. 'We call this a *kum-sitz*, a come-and-sit-down,' Chaim said, then he went on: 'It's the story of the lion and the fox. You come from a terrible world. We know it very little: from the stories of our fathers, and from what we've seen on our missions; but we know that each of you is alive through some miracle, and we know you've left Gehenna behind you. You and we have fought the same enemy, but in two different ways. You had to do it on your own; you had to invent everything, defense, arms, allies, strategy. We were luckier; we were trained, organized, part of a big army. We didn't have enemies on our sides, but only facing us; we didn't have to conquer our weapons, they were issued to us, and we were taught to use them. We have had hard battles, but behind us there were the rear lines, kitchens, infirmaries, and a country that hailed us as liberators. In this country, your weapons will be of no use to you anymore.'

'Why won't they be of use to us?' Mottel asked. 'And how is this country different from the other countries? We're foreigners here, the same as everywhere else; in fact we're more foreign here than in Russia or Poland, and a foreigner is an enemy.'

'Italy is an odd country,' Chaim said. 'It takes a long time to understand the Italians, and not even we, who've come all the way up Italy, from Brindisi to the Alps, have yet managed to understand it clearly; but one thing is certain, in Italy foreigners aren't enemies. You'd think the Italians are more enemies to one another than to foreigners: it's strange, but it's true. Maybe this comes from the fact that the Italians don't like laws, and since Mussolini's laws, also his policy and his propaganda, condemned foreigners, for this very reason the Italians helped them. The Italians don't like laws; in fact they like disobeying them; it's their game, like the Russians' game of chess. They like to cheat; they dislike being cheated, but only up to a point. When someone cheats them, they think: look how smart he is, smarter than me. And they don't plan their vengeance, but at most another game, to get their own back, Like chess, in fact.'

'Then they'll cheat us too,' Line said.

'That's probable, but it's the only risk you run. That's why I said your weapons won't be of use. But at this point I must tell you the strangest thing of all: the Italians have proved to be the friends of all foreigners, but they haven't been as friendly with any as with the Palestine Brigade.'

'Maybe they didn't realize you were Jews,' Mendel said.

'Of course, they realized, and for that matter we made no secret of it. They helped us not in spite of the fact we're Jews, but *because* of it. They also helped their own Jews; when the

Germans occupied Italy, they made every effort they could to capture the Italian Jews, but they caught and killed only a fifth. All the others found refuge in Christians' houses, and not only the Italian Jews, but many foreign Jews who had sought refuge in Italy.'

'Maybe this happened because the Italians are good Christians,' Mendel ventured again.

'That may be, too,' Chaim said, scratching his brow, 'but I'm not sure of it. Even as Christians, the Italians are odd. They go to Mass, but they curse. They ask favors of the Madonna and the saints, but they don't seem to believe much in God. They know the Ten Commandments by heart, but at most they observe two or three. I believe they help those in need because they're good people, who have suffered a lot, and who know that those who suffer should be helped.'

'The Poles have also suffered a lot, but . . .'

'I don't know what to say to you: there could be a dozen reasons, all good and all bad. But there's one thing you should know: Italian Jews are as odd as the Catholics. They don't speak Yiddish, in fact they don't even know what Yiddish is. They only speak Italian; or rather, the Jews of Rome speak Roman, the Jews of Venice speak Venetian, and so on. They dress like everybody else, they have the same face as everybody else . . .'

'Then how can they be told from the Christians when they walk along the street?'

'They can't, that's the point. Isn't that an unusual country? For that matter there aren't very many of them; the Christians don't give them any thought, and they themselves don't think much about being Jews. In Italy there's never been a pogrom, not even when the Roman Church told the Christians to despise the Jews and accused them all of being usurers, not even when Mussolini decreed the racial laws, not even when northern Italy was occupied by the Germans. Nobody in Italy knows what a pogrom is, they don't even know what the word means. It's an oasis, this country. Italian Jews were Fascists when all the Italians were Fascists and applauded Mussolini; and when the Germans came, some escaped to Switzerland, some became partisans, but the majority remained hidden in the city or the countryside; and very few were discovered or reported, even though the Germans promised a lot of money to anyone who collaborated. There, this is the country you're entering: a country of good people, who don't much like war, who like confusing issues; and since, to get to Palestine, we have to cheat the English, this is really the ideal place. It's like a dock just in the right place, as if it had been put there especially for us.'

PRIMO LEVI

ITALIAN JOURNEY

It was written, then, on my page in the Book of Fate that, at five in the afternoon of the twenty-eight day of September in the year 1786, I should see Venice for the first time as I entered this beautiful island-city, this beaver-republic. So now, thank God, Venice is no longer a mere word to me, an empty name, a state of mind which has so often alarmed me who am the mortal enemy of mere words.

When the first gondola came alongside our boat – this they do to bring passengers who are in a hurry to Venice more quickly – I remembered from early childhood a toy to which I had not given a thought for perhaps twenty years. My father had brought back from his journey to Italy a beautiful model of a gondola; he was very fond of it and, as a special treat, he sometimes allowed me to play with it. When the gondolas appeared their shining steel-sheeted prows and black cages greeted me like old friends.

I have found comfortable lodgings in the Queen of England, not far from the Piazza San Marco. My windows look out on to a narrow canal between high houses; immediately below them is a single-span bridge, and opposite, a narrow, crowded passage. This is where I shall live until my parcel for Germany is ready and I have had my fill of sightseeing, which may be some time. At last I can really enjoy the solitude I have been longing for, because nowhere can one be more alone than in a large crowd through which one pushes one's way, a complete stranger. In all Venice there is probably only one person who knows me, and it is most unlikely that I shall meet him at once.

WOLFGANG GOETHE

ITALIAN HOURS

The Venetian people have little to call their own – little more than the bare privilege of leading their lives in the most beautiful of towns. Their habitations are decayed; their taxes are heavy; their pockets light; their opportunities few. One receives an impression, however, that life presents itself to them with attractions not accounted for in this meagre train of advantages, and that they are on better terms with it than many people who have made a better bargain. They lie in the sunshine; they dabble in the sea; they wear bright rags; they fall into attitudes and harmonies; they assist at an eternal *conversazione*. It is not easy to say that no one would have them other than they are, and it certainly would make an immense difference should they be better fed. The number of persons in Venice who evidently never have enough to eat is painfully large; but it would be more painful if we did not equally perceive that the rich Venetian temperament may bloom upon a dog's allowance. Nature has been kind to it, and sunshine and leisure and conversation and beautiful views form the greater part of its sustenance. It takes a great deal to make a successful American, but to make a happy Venetian takes only a handful of quick sensibility. The Italian people have at once the good and the evil fortune to be conscious of few wants; so that if the civilisation of a society is measured by the number of its needs, as seems to be the common opinion to-day, it is to be feared that the children of the lagoon would make but a poor figure in a set of comparative tables. Not their misery, doubtless, but the way they elude their misery, is what pleases the sentimental tourist, who is gratified by the sight of a beautiful race that lives by the aid of its imagination. The way to enjoy Venice is to follow the example of these people and make the most of simple pleasures. Almost all the pleasures of the place are simple; this may be maintained even under the imputation of ingenious paradox.

There is no simpler pleasure than looking at a fine Titian, unless it be looking at a fine Tintoretto or strolling into St Mark's – abominable the way one falls into the habit – and resting one's light-wearied eyes upon the windowless gloom; or than floating in a gondola or than hanging over a balcony or than taking one's coffee at Florian's. It is of such superficial pastimes that a Venetian day is composed, and the pleasure of the matter is in the motions to which they minister. These are fortunately of the finest – otherwise Venice would be insufferably dull. Reading Ruskin is good; reading the old records is perhaps better; but the best thing of all is simply staying on. The only way to care for Venice as she deserves it is to give her a chance to touch you often – to linger and remain and return.

The danger is that you will not linger enough – a danger of which the author of these lines had known something. It is possible to dislike Venice, and to entertain the sentiment in a responsible and intelligent manner. There are travellers who think the place odious, and those who are not of this opinion often find themselves wishing that the others were only more numerous. The sentimental tourist's sole quarrel with his Venice is that he has too many competitors there. He likes to be alone; to be original; to have (to himself, at least) the air of making discoveries. The Venice of to-day is a vast museum where the little wicket that admits you is perpetually turning and creaking, and you march through the institution with a herd of fellow-gazers. There is nothing left to discover or describe, and originality of attitude is completely impossible. This is often very annoying: you can only turn your back on your impertinent playfellow and curse his want of delicacy. But this is not the fault of Venice; it is the fault of the rest of the world. The fault of Venice is that, though she is easy to admire, she is not easy to live with as you count living in other places. After you have stayed a week and the bloom of novelty has rubbed off you wonder if you can accommodate yourself to the peculiar conditions. Your old habits become impracticable and you find yourself obliged to form new ones of an undesirable and unprofitable character. You are tired of your gondola (or you think you are) and you have seen all the principal pictures and heard the names of the palaces announced a dozen times by your gondolier, who brings them out almost as impressively as if he were an English butler bawling titles into a drawing-room. You have walked several hundred times round the Piazza and bought several bushels of photographs. You have visited the antiquity-mongers whose horrible sign-boards dishonour some of the grandest vistas in the Grand Canal; you have tried the opera and found it very bad; you have bathed at the Lido and found the water flat. You have begun to have a shipboard-feeling – to regard the Piazza as an enormous saloon and the Riva degli Schiavoni as a promenade-deck. You are obstructed and encaged; your desire for space is unsatisfied; you miss your usual exercise. You try to take a walk and you fail, and mean-time, as I say, you have come to regard your gondola as a sort of magnified baby's cradle. You have no desire to be rocked to sleep, though you are sufficiently kept awake by the irritation produced, as you gaze across the shallow lagoon, by the attitude of the perpetual gondolier, with his turned-out toes, his pro-truded chin, his absurdly unscientific stroke. The canals have a horrible smell, and the everlasting Piazza, where you have looked repeatedly at every article in every shop-window and found them all rubbish, where the young Venetians who sell bead bracelets and 'panoramas' are perpetually thrusting their wares at you, where the same tightly-buttoned officers are for ever sucking the same black weeds, at the same empty tables, in front of the same cafés – the Piazza, as I say, has resolved itself into a magnificent tread-mill. This is the state of mind of those shallow enquirers who find Venice all very well for a week; and if in such a state of mind you take your departure, you act with fatal rashness. The loss is your own, moreover; it is not, with all deference to your personal attractions, that of your companions who remain behind; for though there are some disagreeable things in Venice there is nothing so disagreeable as the visitors. The conditions are peculiar, but your intolerance of them evaporates before it has had time to become a prejudice. When you have called for the bill to go, pay it and remain, and you will find on the morrow that you are deeply attached to Venice. It is by living there from day to day that you feel the fulness of her charms; that you invite her exquisite influence to sink into your spirit. The creature varies like a nervous woman, whom you know only when you know all the aspects of her beauty. She has high spirits or low, she is pale or red, grey or pink, cold or warm, fresh or wan, according to the weather or the hour. She is always interesting and almost always sad; but she has a thousand occasional graces and is always liable to happy accidents. You become extraordinarily fond of these things; you count upon them; they make part of your life. Tenderly fond you become; there is something indefinable in those depths of personal acquaintance that gradually establish themselves. The place seems to personify itself, to become human and sentient and conscious of your affection. You desire to embrace it, to caress it, to possess it; and finally a soft sense of possession grows up and your visit becomes a perpetual love-affair.

You soon recognise that it is not only the many-twinkling lagoon you behold from a habitation on the Riva; you see a little of everything Venetian. Straight across, before my windows, rose the great pink mass of San Giorgio Maggiore, which has for an ugly Palladian church a success beyond all reason. It is a success of position, of colour, of the immense detached Campanile, tipped with a tall gold angel. I know not whether it is because San Giorgio is so grandly conspicuous, with a great deal of worn, faded-looking brickwork; but for many persons the whole place has a kind of suffusion of rosiness. Asked what may be the leading colour in the Venetian concert, we should inveterately say Pink, and yet without remembering after all that this elegant hue occurs very often. It is a faint, shimmering, airy, watery pink; the bright sea-light seems to flush with it and the pale whiteish-green of lagoon and canal drink it in. There is indeed a great deal of very evident brickwork, which is never fresh or loud in colour, but always burnt out, as it were, always exquisitely mild.

Certain little mental pictures rise before the collector of memories at the simple mention, written or spoken, of the places he has loved. When I hear, when I see, the magical name I have written above these pages, it is not of the great Square that I think, with its strange basilica and its high arcades, nor of the wide mouth of the Grand Canal, with the stately steps and the well-poised Dome of the Salute; it is not of the low lagoon, nor the sweet Piazzetta, nor the dark chambers of St Mark's. I simply see a narrow canal in the heart of the city – a patch of green water and a surface of pink wall. The gondola moves slowly; it gives a great smooth swerve, passes under a bridge, and the gondolier's cry, carried over the quiet water, makes a kind of splash in the stillness. A girl crosses the little bridge, which has an arch like a camel's back, with an old shawl on her head, which makes her characteristic and charming; you see her against the sky as you float beneath. The pink of the old wall seems to fill the whole place; it sinks even into the opaque water. Behind the wall is a garden, out of which the long arm of a white June rose – the roses of Venice are splendid – has flung itself by way of spontaneous ornament. On the other side of this small water-way is a great shabby face of Gothic windows and balconies – balconies in which dirty clothes are hung and under which a cavernous-looking doorway opens from a low flight of slimy water-steps. It is very hot and still, the canal has a queer smell, and the whole place is enchanting.

It is poor work, however, talking about the colour of things in Venice. The fond spectator is perpetually looking at it from his window, when he is not floating about with that delightful sense of being for the moment a part of it, which any gentleman in a gondola is free to entertain. Venetian windows and balconies are a dreadful lure, and while you rest your elbows on these cushioned ledges the precious hours fly away. But in truth

Venice isn't in fair weather a place for concentration of mind. The effort required for sitting down to a writing-table is heroic, and the brightest pages of MS. looks dull beside the brilliancy of your *milieu.* All nature beckons you forth and murmurs to you sophistically that such hours should be devoted to collecting impressions. Afterwards, in ugly places, at unprivileged times, you can convert your impressions into prose. Fortunately for the present proser the weather wasn't always fine; the first month was wet and windy, and it was better to judge of the matter from an open casement than to respond to the advances of persuasive gondoliers. Later it all turned warm. The lagoon was streaked with odd currents, which played across it like huge smooth finger-marks. The gondolas multiplied and spotted it all over; every gondola and gondolier looking, at a distance, precisely like every other.

There is something strange and fascinating in this mysterious impersonality of the gondola. It has an identity when you are in it, but, thanks to their all being of the same size, shape and colour, and of the same deportment and gait, it has none, or as little as possible, as you see it pass before you. From my windows on the Riva there was always the same silhouette – the long, black, slender skiff, lifting its head and throwing it back a little, moving yet seeming not to move, with the grotesquely-graceful figure on the poop. This figure inclines, as may be, more to the graceful or the grotesque – standing in the 'second position' of the dancing-master, but indulging from the waist upward in a freedom of movement which that functionary would deprecate. One may say as a general thing that there is something rather awkward in the movement of even the most graceful gondolier, and something graceful in the movement of the most awkward.

May in Venice is better than April, but June is best of all. Then the days are hot, but not too hot, and the nights are more beautiful than the days. Then Venice is rosier than ever in the morning and more golden than ever as the day descends. She seems to expand and evaporate, to multiply all her reflections and iridescences. Then the life of her people and the strangeness of her constitution become a perpetual comedy, or at least a perpetual drama. Then the gondola is your sole habitation, and you spend days between sea and sky.

Venetian life in the large old sense, has long since come to an end, and the essential present character of the most melancholy of cities resides simply in its being the most beautiful of tombs. Nowhere else has the past been laid to rest with such tenderness, such a sadness of resignation and remembrance.

HENRY JAMES

Is there anyone but must repress a secret thrill on arriving in Venice for the first time – or returning thither after long absence – and stepping into a Venetian gondola? That singular conveyance, come down unchanged from ballad times, black as nothing else on earth except a coffin – what pictures it calls up of lawless, silent adventures in the plashing night; or even more, what visions of death itself, the bier and solemn rites and last soundless voyage! And has anyone remarked that the seat in such a bark, the armchair lacquered in coffin-black and dully upholstered, is the softest, most luxurious, most relaxing seat in the world? Aschenbach realized it when he had let himself down at the gondolier's feet, opposite his luggage, which lay neatly composed on the vessel's beak. The rowers still gestured fiercely; he heard their harsh, incoherent tones. But the strange stillness of the water-city seemed to take up their voices gently, to dis-embody and scatter them over the sea. It was warm here in the harbour. The lukewarm air of the sirocco breathed upon him, he leaned back among his cushions and gave himself to the yielding element, closing his eyes for the very pleasure in an indolence as unaccustomed as sweet. 'The trip will be short,' he thought, and wished it might last forever.

From *Death in Venice*, THOMAS MANN

THE NEW ITALIANS

Everyone knows something of Italy. Our collective cultural bag-gage is festooned with labels from Rome and Florence. Italy is Roman law and Renaissance rules of perspective, it is the uni-versal Church and the roots of Western civilization. Italy is a summer's lease of a Tuscan villa. It is swifts – visitors from the South – screaming and wheeling over terracotta roofs in Trastavere. It is sunshine and blue skies, extra-virgin olive oil and olive-skinned lovelies entangled on a Vespa. It is the world's best-dressed people, and cappuccino in the Mecca of Mocha. Italians can also have execrable taste. As a sign of their new wealth, they are the biggest importers of Persian carpets in Europe, but they prefer garish, floral patterns to more muted tribal designs. Once upon a time Italy was a place where rich Northern Europeans found their money went a long way. But fifteen years of high inflation have made Italy today one of the more expensive countries in Europe.

Italy as a modern state with the same-sized population as the United Kingdom or France, is much less well understood. Luigi Barzini, whose *The Italians* published in 1964 remains a timeless portrayal of the feats and foibles of his countrymen, warned about the difficulties in seeking to decipher the Italian puzzle. 'Italy,' he wrote, 'is universally considered a particularly unpredictable and deceptive country. Some people even believe that this is the only absolute certain thing about it. They are, of course, right some of the time, but also wrong as often. There are no sure guides to what Italy is and what it might do next. Italians themselves are almost always baffled by their own behaviour. The only people who have no doubts and hold very definite and clear ideas about the country and its inhabitants are foreigners who streak through it in a few days.'

My brief was to write a personal attempt to come to understand Italy and its people. What struck me, as it has struck others, was how the Italians manage to appear both rich and happy, to have money and know how to spend it with such, well, with what else but such *brio* and *gusto*? This was the question to which above all others I sought an answer. Now I know that, underneath, the Italians are not so happy. How else does one account for the high incidence of suicides, and the rising numbers seeking psychiatric help? The huge drugs problem was a further sign of escapism, mainly of young people seeking ways of not facing up to reality. But on the surface the Italians seem to have the best way of life in the world. Was the reason for this lifestyle the Italian model of an apparently anarchic system of government? Could this be replicated elsewhere, or was the Italian way of life confined to the peninsula?

Many others have made the same investigation at different times. Hans Magnus Enzensberger, the most perspicacious observer of the differences within the great European family, was dismissive of Italy as the laboratory of the post-modern.

The Germans, the English, or the Finns could not act like the Italians even if they wanted to. They're not astute enough, not cynical enough, not talented enough: they're too stubborn, too set in their ways, too amateurish, too inhibited. They've invested too much energy in their well-ordered systems, delegated too many resources, responsibilities, and hopes to the state. They're out of practice when it comes to relying on their own initiative and can't say 'Me and my clan, my family, my shop, we'll manage – and all the rest can go to hell.'

We'll never go so far as the Italians. Only when we're left with no other choice will we, somehow or other, borrow this or that number from the Italian repertoire. However, we will continue to regard Model Italy, which is not a model at all but an unpredictable, productive, fantastic tumult, with mixed feelings of fear and admiration, dismay and envy.

Italy is a country where laws are turned upside down. Elsewhere, power tends to corrupt, and absolute power corrupts absolutely. In Italy the absence of absolute power has not prevented its absolute corruption. Italian political life is about co-operation and consensus. As Gore Vidal observed, the genius of America was to separate State from Religion. The genius of Italy was to separate the State from the People.

Some argue that Italians thrive on the absence of strong central government, rather than despite it (local and regional government in the North is often quite good). Alternatively, they prosper despite their politicians, rather than because of them. It is a question that ceased to be academic. For as Italy started the difficult and painful process of reform, the question had to be asked again: What had led them to their current pass? Was it the system, or the Italians themselves?

It is a cliché to describe Italy as a country made up of several quite different countries: geographically, topographically, culturally, economically. It is one of those fortunate countries blessed with diversity in climate and landscape, where you can ski in the mountains and swim in the sea, virtually in the same day. Because it is long like a boot, it passes through many different temperature zones. The history of the peninsula, too, accounts in large part for why the North feels closer to Middle Europe, and the South seems more part of the Levant.

The regional variations of Italian life find fullest flavour in the cuisine. One of the most celebrated writers on the food of Italy, Marcella Hazan, states without any leavening that:

The first useful thing to know about Italian cooking is that as such it actually doesn't exist. 'Italian cooking' is an expression of convenience rarely used by Italians. The cooking of Italy is really the cooking of its regions, regions that until 1861 were separate, independent, and usually hostile states. They submitted to different rules, they were protected by sovereign armies and navies, and they developed their own cultural traditions and, of course, their own special and distinct approaches to food . . .

Tuscany's whole approach to the preparation of food is in such sharp contrast to that of Bologna that their differences seem to sum up two main and contrary manifestations of Italian character. Out of the abundance of the Bolognese kitchen comes cooking that is exuberant, prodigal with precious ingredients, and wholly baroque in its restless exploration of every agreeable combination of texture and flavour. The Florentine, careful and calculating, is a man who knows the measure of all things and his cooking is an austerely composed play upon essential and unadorned themes. Bologna will sauté veal in butter, stuff it with the finest mountain ham, coat it with aged Parmesan, simmer it in sauce, and smother it with the costliest truffles. Florence takes a T-bone steak of noble size and grills it quickly over the blazing fire, adding nothing but the aroma of freshly ground pepper and olive oil. Both are triumphs. (From the introduction to *The Classic Italian Cookbook*)

That regions are different because of their histories is not contested. The great fault line has always been between the North and the South. Where this fault line lies is a matter of often heated discussion. Some place it along the Germans' Gothic line of defence against the Allied advance, between Rome and

Florence. Northerners will joke that Garibaldi did not unify Italy, but dismembered Africa. Does Egypt begin (they ask) at Rome, or Orvieto, or Florence?

CHARLES RICHARDS

THE LETTERS OF LORD BYRON

To Thomas Moore
Verona, November 6, 1816

My dear Moore,

Your letter, written before my departure from England, and addressed to me in London, only reached me recently. Since that period, I have been over that part of Europe which I had not already seen. About a month since, I crossed the Alps from Switzerland to Milan, which I left a few days ago, and am thus far on my way to Venice, where I shall probably winter . . .

We moved to-day over the frontier to Verona, by a road suspected of thieves, – 'the wise *convey* it call', – but without molestation. I shall remain here a day or two to gape at the usual marvels, – amphitheatre, paintings, and all that time-tax of travel, – though Catullus, Claudian, and Shakespeare have done more for Verona than it ever did for itself. They still pretend to show, I believe, 'the tomb of all the Capulets' – we shall see.

Among many things in Milan, one pleased me particularly, viz. the correspondence (in the prettiest love-letters in the world) of Lucretia Borgia with Cardinal Bembo, (who, *you say*, made a very good cardinal,) and a lock of her hair, and some Spanish verses of hers, – the lock very fair and beautiful. I took one single hair of it as a relic, and wished solely to get a copy of one or two of the letters; but it is prohibited: that I don't mind; but it was impracticable; and so I only got some of them by heart. They are kept in the Ambrosian Library, which I often visited to look them over – to the scandal of the librarian, who wanted to enlighten me with sundry valuable MSS., classical, philosophical, and pious. But I stick to the Pope's daughter and wish myself a cardinal.

My health is very endurable, except that I am subject to casual giddiness and faintnesses, which is so like a fine lady, that I am rather ashamed of the disorder . . .

The state of morals in these parts is in some sort lax. A mother and son were pointed out at the theatre, as being pronounced by the Milanese world to be of the Theban dynasty – but this was all. The narrator (one of the first men in Milan) seemed to be not sufficiently scandalized by the taste or the tie. All society in Milan is carried on at the opera: they have private boxes, where they play at cards, or talk, or anything else; but (except for the casino) there are no open houses, or balls, etc., etc.

The peasant girls have all very fine dark eyes, and many of them are beautiful. There are also two dead bodies in fine preservation – one Saint Carlo Boromeo, at Milan; the other not a saint but a chief named Visconti, at Monza – both of which appeared very agreeable. In one of the

Boromean isles (the Isola bella), there is a large laurel – the largest known – on which Buonaparte, staying there just before the battle of Marengo, carved with his knife the word 'Battaglia'. I saw the letters, now half worn out and partly erased.

Excuse this tedious letter. To be tiresome is the privilege of old age and absence; I avail myself of the latter, and the former I have anticipated. If I do not speak to you of my own affairs, it is not from want of confidence, but to spare you and myself. My day is over – what then? – I have had it. To be sure, I have shortened it; and if I had done as much by this letter, it would have been as well. But you will forgive that, if not the other faults of

Yours ever and most affectionately,

B.

P.S. I have been over Verona. The amphitheatre is wonderful – beats even Greece. Of the truth of Juliet's story they seem tenacious to a degree, insisting on the fact – giving a date (1303) and showing a tomb. It is a plain, open, and partly decayed sarcophagus, with withered leaves in it, in a wild and desolate conventual garden, once a cemetery, now ruined to the very graves. The situation struck me as very appropriate to the legend, being as blighted as their love. I have brought away a few pieces of the granite, to give to my daughter and my nieces.

Dear Sir,

It is some months since I have heard from or of you – I think, not since I left Diodati. From Milan I wrote once or twice; but have been here some little time, and intend to pass the winter without removing. I was much pleased with the Lago di Garda, and with Verona, particularly the amphitheatre, and the sarcophagus in a Convent garden, which they show as Juliet's: they insist on the *truth* of her history. Since my arrival at Venice, the lady of the Austrian governor told me that between Verona and Vicenza there are still ruins of the castle of the *Montecchi*, and a chapel once appertaining to the Capulets. Romeo seems to have been of Vicenza by the tradition; but I was a good deal surprised to find so firm a faith in Bandello's novel, which seems really to have been founded on fact.

Venice pleases me as much as I expected, and I expected much. It is one of those places which I know before I see them, and has always haunted me the most after the East. I like the gloomy gaiety of their gondolas, and the silence of their canals. I do not even dislike the evident decay of the city, though I regret the singularity of its vanished costume; however, there is much still left; the Carnival, too, is coming.

St. Mark's, and indeed Venice, is most alive at night. The theatres are not open till *nine*, and the society is proportionably late. All this is to my taste; but most of your countrymen miss and regret the rattle of hackney carriages, without which they can't sleep.

I have got remarkably good apartments in a private
house: I see something of the inhabitants (having had a
good many letters to some of them); I have got my gondola;
I read a little, and luckily could speak Italian (more fluently
though than accurately) long ago. I am studying, out of
curiosity, the *Venetian* dialect, which is vary naive, and soft,
and peculiar, though not at all classical; I go out frequently,
and am in very good contentment.

The general race of women appear to be handsome; but
in Italy, as on almost all the Continent, the highest orders
are by no means a well-looking generation, and indeed
reckoned by their countrymen very much otherwise. Some
are exceptions, but most of them are as ugly as Virtue
herself.

I suppose you have a world of works passing through
your process for next year? When does Moore's poem
appear? I sent a letter for him, addressed to your care, the
other day.

So Mr Frere is married; and you tell me in a former
letter that he had 'nearly forgotten that he was so'. He is
fortunate.

Yours ever, and very truly,
B.

To Thomas Moore
Venice, March 25, 1817

I have been very ill with a slow fever, which at last took to
flying, and became as quick as need be. But, at length, after
a week of half-delirium, burning skin, thirst, hot headache,

horrible pulsation, and no sleep, by the blessing of barley water, and refusing to see any physician, I recovered. It is an epidemic of the place, which is annual, and visits strangers.

I have not the least idea where I am going, nor what I am to do. I wished to have gone to Rome; but at present it is pestilent with English – a parcel of staring boobies, who go about gaping and wishing to be at once cheap and magnificent. A man is a fool now who travels in France or Italy, till this tribe of wretches is swept home again. In two or three years the first rush will be over, and the Continent will be roomy and agreeable.

I stayed at Venice chiefly because it is not one of their 'dens of thieves'; and here they but pause and pass . . .

I am still in love, – which is a dreadful drawback in quitting a place, and I can't stay at Venice much longer. What I shall do on this point I don't know. The girl means to go with me, but I do not like this for her own sake . . .

The Italian ethics are the most singular ever met with, the perversion, not only of action, but of reasoning, is singular in the women. It is not that they do not consider the thing itself as wrong, and very wrong, but *love* (the *sentiment* of love) is not merely an excuse for it, but makes it an *actual virtue*, provided it is disinterested, and not a *caprice*, and is confined to one object. They have awful notions of constancy; for I have seen some ancient figures of eighty pointed out as *Amorosi* of forty, fifty, and sixty years' standing. I can't say I have ever seen a husband and wife so coupled.

Ever, etc.

To John Murray
Foligno, April 26, 1817

At Florence I remained but a day, having a hurry for
Rome, to which I am thus far advanced. However, I went
to the two galleries, from which one returns drunk with
beauty . . .

I also went to the Medici chapel – fine frippery in great
slabs of various expensive stones, to commemorate fifty
rotten and forgotten carcases. It is unfinished and will
remain so.

To John Murray
Venice, June 4, 1817

Dear Sir,

I was delighted with Rome, and was on horseback all
round it many hours daily, besides in it the rest of my time,
bothering over its marvels. I excursed and skirted the
country round to Alba, Tivoli, Frascati, Licenza, etc., etc.;
besides, I visited twice the Fall of Terni, which beats
everything. On my way back, close to the temple by its
banks, I got some famous trout out of the river
Clitumnus – the prettiest little stream in all poesy, near the
first post from Foligno and Spoletta. – I did not stay at
Florence, being anxious to get home to Venice, and having
already seen the galleries and other sights. I left my
commendatory letters the evening before I went, so I saw
nobody . . .

I forgot to tell you that at Bologna (which is celebrated
for producing popes, painters, and sausages) I saw an

anatomical gallery, where there is a deal of waxwork, in which . . .

In a few days I go to my Villegiatura, in a casino near the Brenta, a few miles only on the main land. I have determined on another year, and *many years* of residence if I can compass them . . .

Ever yours truly,

B.

To Lady Byron
Ravenna, July 20th, 1819

The date of my letter, indeed my letter itself, may surprise you, but I left Venice in the beginning of June, and came down into Romagna; there is the famous forest of Boccaccio's Story and Dryden's fable hardby, the Adriatic not far distant, and the Sepulchre of Dante within the walls. I am just going to take a Canter (for I have resumed my Tartar habits since I left England) in the cool of the Evening, and in the shadow of the forest until the Ave Maria. I have got both my saddle and Carriage horses with me, and I don't spare them, in the cooler part of the day. But I shall probably return to Venice in a short time. Ravenna itself preserves perhaps more of the old Italian manners than any City in Italy. It is out of the way of travellers and armies, and thus they have retained more of their originality. They make love a great deal, and assassinate a little.

WALKS IN ROME

At the foot of the Pyramid is the *Old Protestant Cemetery*, a lovely spot, now closed. Here is the grave of Keats, with the inscription:

> This grave contains all that was mortal of a young English poet, who, on his death-bed, in the bitterness of his heart at the malicious power of his enemies, desired these words to be engraved on his tomb-stone: 'Here lies one whose name was writ in water.' February 24, 1821

The *New Burial* ground was opened in 1825. It extends for some distance along the slope of the hill under the old Aurelian Wall, and is beautifully shaded by cypresses, and carpeted with violets. Amid the forest of tombs we may notice that which contains the heart of Shelley (his body having been burnt upon the shore of Lerici, where it was thrown up by the sea), inscribed:

> Percy Bysshe Shelley, Cor Cordium. Natus IV Aug.
> MDCCXCIL Obiit VIII Jul. MDCCCXXIL
> 'Nothing of him that doth fade
> But doth suffer a sea change
> Into something rich and strange'

REV. AUGUSTUS HARE

[Trelawny obtained permission, through the good offices of the British minister at Florence, to take possession of the bodies of

Shelley and Williams. He then arranged for two separate cremations, that of Williams taking place first, and that of Shelley on the following day, 16 August.]

Three white wands had been stuck in the sand to mark the Poet's grave, but as they were at some distance from each other, we had to cut a trench thirty yards in length, in line of the sticks, to ascertain the exact spot, and it was nearly an hour before we came upon the grave.

In the mean time Byron and Leigh Hunt arrived in the carriage, attended by soldiers, and the Health Officer, as before. The lonely and grand scenery that surrounded us so exactly harmonised with Shelley's genius, that I could imagine his spirit soaring over us. The sea, with the islands of Gorgona, Capraia, and Elba, was before us; old battlemented watchtowers stretched along the coast, backed by the marble-crested Apennines glistening in the sun, picturesque from their diversified outlines, and not a human dwelling in sight. As I thought of the delight Shelley felt in such scenes of loneliness and grandeur while living, I felt we were no better than a herd of wolves or a pack of wild dogs, in tearing out his battered and naked body from the pure yellow sand that lay so lightly over it, to drag him back to the light of day; but the dead have no voice, nor had I the power to check the sacrilege – the work went on silently in the deep and unresisting sand. Not a word was spoken, for the Italians have a touch of sentiment, and their feelings are easily excited into sympathy. Even Byron was silent and thoughtful. We were startled and drawn together by a dull hollow sound that followed the blow of a mattock; the iron had struck a skull, and the body was soon recovered. Lime had been strewn on it; this, or decomposition, had the effect of staining it of a dark and ghastly indigo colour. Byron asked me to preserve the skull for him; but remembering that he had formerly used one as a drinking-cup, I was determined Shelley's should not be so profaned. The limbs did not separate from the trunk, as in the case of William's body, so that the corpse was removed entire into the furnace. I had taken the precaution of having more and larger pieces of timber, in consequence of my experience of the day before of the difficulty of consuming a corpse in the open air with our apparatus. After the fire was well kindled we repeated the ceremony of the previous day; and more wine was poured over Shelley's dead body than he had consumed during his life. This with the oil and salt made the yellow flames glisten and quiver. The heat from the sun and fire was so intense that the atmosphere was tremulous and wavy. The corpse fell open and the heart was laid bare. The frontal bone of the skull, where it had been struck with the mattock, fell off; and, as the back of the head rested on the red-hot bottom bars of the furnace, the brains literally seethed, bubbled, and boiled as in a cauldron, for a very long time.

Byron could not face this scene, he withdrew to the beach and swam off to the *Bolivar*. Leigh Hunt remained in the carriage. The fire was so fierce as to produce a white heat on the iron, and to reduce its contents to grey ashes. The only portions that were not consumed were some fragments of bones, the jaw, and the skull, but what surprised us all, was that the heart remained entire. In snatching this relic from the fiery furnace, my hand was severely burnt; and had anyone seen me do the act I should have been put in quarantine.

After cooling the iron machine in the sea, I collected the human ashes and placed them in a box, which I took on board the *Bolivar*. Byron and Hunt retraced their steps to their home, and the officers and soldiers returned to their quarters . . .

EDWARD TRELAWNY

To Europe. 1948

Standing very still you could hear a harp. We climbed the wall, and there, among the burning rain-drenched flowers of the castle's garden, sat four mysterious figures, a young man who thumbed a hand harp and three rusted old men who were dressed in patched-together black; how stark they were against the storm-green air. And they were eating figs, those Italian figs so fat the juice ran out of their mouths. At the garden's edge lay the marble shore of Lago di Garda, its waters swarming in the wind, and I knew then I would always be afraid to swim there, for, like distortions beyond the beauty of ivy-glass, Gothic creatures must move in the depths of water so ominously clear. One of the old men tossed too far a fig peel and a trio of swans, thus disturbed, rustled the reeds of the waterway.

D. jumped off the wall and gestured for me to join him, but I couldn't, not quite then: because suddenly it was true and I wanted the trueness of it to last a moment longer – I could never feel it so absolutely again, even the movement of a leaf and it would be lost, precisely as a cough would forever ruin Tourel's high note. And what was this truth? Only the truth of justification; a castle, swans and a boy with a harp, for all the world out of a childhood storybook before the prince had entered or the witch had cast her spell.

It was right that I had gone to Europe, if only because I could look again and wonder. Past certain ages or certain wisdoms it is very difficult to look with wonder; it is best done when one is a child; after that, and if you are lucky, you will find a bridge of childhood and walk across it. Going to Europe was like that. It was a bridge of childhood, one that led over the seas and through the forests straight into my imagination's earliest landscapes. One way or another I had gone to a good many places, from Mexico to Maine – and then to think I had to go all the way to Europe to go back to my hometown, my fire and room where stories and legends seemed always to live beyond the limits of our town. And that is where the legends were: in the harp, the castle, the rustling of the swans.

A rather mad bus ride that day had brought us from Venice to Sirmione, an enchanted, infinitesimal village on the tip of a peninsula jutting into Lago di Garda, bluest, saddest, most silent, most beautiful of Italian lakes. Had it not been for the gruesome circumstances of Lucia, I doubt that we should have left Venice. I was perfectly happy there, except of course that it is incredibly noisy: not ordinary city noise, but ceaseless argument of human voices, scudding oars, running feet. It was once suggested that Oscar Wilde retire there from the world. 'And become a monument for tourists?' he asked.

It was excellent advice, however, and others than Oscar have taken it; in the palazzos along the Grand Canal there are colonies of persons who haven't shown themselves publicly in a number of decades. Most intriguing of these was a Swedish countess whose servants fetched fruit for her in a black gondola trimmed with silver bells; their tinkling made a music atmospheric but eerie. Still, Lucia so persecuted us we were forced to flee. A muscular girl, exceptionally tall for an Italian and smelling always of wretched condiment oils, she was the leader of a band of juvenile gangsters, displaced roaming youths who had flocked north for the Venetian season. They could be delightful, some of them, even though they sold cigarettes that contained more hay than tobacco, even though they would short-circuit you on a currency exchange. The business with Lucia began one day in the Piazza San Marco.

She came up and asked us for a cigarette; whereupon D., whose heart doesn't know that we are off the gold standard, gave her a whole package of Chesterfields. Never were two people more completely adopted. Which at first was quite pleasant. Lucia shadowed us wherever we went, abundantly giving us the benefits of her wisdom and protection. But there were frequent embarrassments; for one thing, we were always being turned out of the more elegant shops because of her overwrought haggling with the proprietors; then, too, she was so excessively jealous that it was impossible for us to have any contact with anyone else whatever: we chanced once to meet in the Piazza a harmless and respectable young woman who had been with us in the carriage from Milan. 'Attention!' said Lucia in that hoarse voice of hers. 'Attention!' and proceeded almost to persuade us that this was a lady of infamous past and shameless future. On another occasion D. gave one of her cohorts a dollar watch which he had much admired. Lucia was furious; the next time we saw her she had the watch suspended on a cord around her neck, and it was said the young man had left overnight for Trieste.

Lucia had a habit of appearing in our hotel at any hour that pleased her (she lived no place that we could divine); scarcely sixteen, she would sit herself down, drain a whole bottle of Strega, smoke all the cigarettes she could lay hold of, then fall into an exhausted sleep; only when she slept did her face resemble a child's. But then one dreadful day the hotel manager stopped her in the lobby and told her that she could no longer visit our rooms. It was, he said, an insupportable scandal. So Lucia, rounding up a dozen of her more brutish companions, laid such siege to the hotel that it was necessary to bring down the iron shutters over the doors and call the *carabiniere*. After that we did our best to avoid her.

But to avoid anyone in Venice is much the same as playing hide-and-seek in a one-room apartment, for there was never a city more compactly composed. It is like a museum with carnivalesque overtones, a vast palace that seems to have no doors, all things connected, one leading into another. Over and over in a day the same faces repeated like prepositions in a long sentence: turn a corner, and there was Lucia, the dollar watch dangling between her breasts. She was so in love with D. But presently she turned on us with that intensity of the wounded; perhaps we deserved it, but it was unendurable. Like clouds of gnats her gang would trail us across the piazza spitting invective;

if we sat down for a drink, they would gather in the dark beyond the table and shout outrageous jokes. Half the time we didn't know what they were saying, though it was apparent that everyone else did. Lucia herself did not overtly contribute to this persecution; she remained aloof, directing her operations at a distance. So at last we decided to leave Venice. Lucia knew this. Her spies were everywhere. The morning we left it was raining; just as our gondola slipped into the water, a little crazy-eyed boy appeared and threw us a bundle wrapped in newspaper. D. pulled the paper apart. Inside there was a dead yellow cat, and around its throat there was tied the dollar watch. It gave you a feeling of endless falling. And then suddenly we saw her. Lucia. She was standing alone on one of the little canal bridges, and she was so far hunched over the railing it looked as if she were gong to fall. *Perdonami*, she cried, *ma t'amo* ('forgive me, but I love you.')

In London a young artist said to me, 'How wonderful it must be for an American traveling in Europe for the first time; you can never be a part of it, so none of the pain is yours, you will never have to endure it – yes, for you there is only beauty.'

Not understanding what he meant, I resented this; but later, after some months in France and Italy, I saw that he was right: I was not a part of Europe, I never could be. Safe, I could leave when I wanted to, and for me there was only the honeyed, hallowed air of beauty. But it was not so wonderful as the young man had imagined; it was desperate to feel that one could never be a part of moments so moving, that always one would be isolated from this landscape and these people; and then gradually

I realized I did not have to be a part of it; rather, it could be a part of me. The sudden garden, opera night, wild children snatching flowers and running up a darkening street, a wreath for the dead and nuns in noon light, music from the piazza, a Paris pianola and fireworks on La Grande Nuit, the heart-shaking surprise of mountain visions and water views (lakes like green wine in the chalice of volcanoes, the Mediterranean flickering at the bottoms of cliffs), forsaken far-off towers falling in twilight and candles igniting the jeweled corpses of St Zeno of Verona – all a part of me, elements for the making of my own perspective.

ISCHIA. 1949

I forget why we came here: Ischia. It was being very much talked about, though few people seemed actually to have seen it – except, perhaps, as a jagged blue shadow glimpsed across the water from the heights of its celebrated neighbor, Capri. Some people advised against Ischia and, as I remember, they gave rather spooky reasons. You realize that there is an active volcano? And do you know about the plane? A plane, flying a regular flight between Cairo and Rome, crashed on top an Ischian mountain; there were three survivors, but no one ever saw them alive, for they were stoned to death by goatheards intent on looting the wreckage.

Consequently, we watched the chalky façade of Naples fade with mixed anticipation. It was a classic day, a little cold for southern Italy in March, but crisp and lofty as a kite, and the *Principessa* spanked across the bay like a sassy dolphin. It is a small civilized boat with a tiny bar and a somewhat *outré* clientele: convicts on their way to the prison island of Procida or, at the opposite extreme, young men about to enter the monastery on Ischia. Of course, there are less dramatic passengers – islanders who have been shopping in Naples; here and there a foreigner – extraordinarily few, however: Capri is the tourist catch-all.

Islands are like ships at permanent anchor. To set foot on one is like starting up a gangplank: one is seized by the same feeling of charmed suspension – it seems nothing unkind or vulgar can happen to you; and as the *Principessa* eased into the cove-like harbour of Porto d'Ischia it seemed, seeing the pale, peeling ice-cream colors of the waterfront, as intimate and satisfying as one's own heartbeat. In the wrangle of disembarking, I dropped and broke my watch – an outrageous bit of symbolism, too pointed. At a glance it was plain that Ischia was no place for the rush of hours, islands never are.

I suppose you might say that Porto is the capital of Ischia; at any rate, it is the largest town and even rather fashionable. Most people who visit the island seldom stray from there, for there are several superior hotels, excellent beaches and, perched in the offing like a giant hawk, the Renaissance castle of Vittoria Colonna. The three other fair-sized towns are more rugged. These are: Lacco Ameno, Cassamiciola and, at the farthest end of the island, Forio. It was in Forio that we planned to settle.

We drove there through a green twilight and under a sky of early stars. The road passed high above the sea, where fishing boats, lighted with torches, crawled below like brilliant water-spiders. Furry little bats skimmed in the dusk; *buena séra, buena séra*, dim evening voices called along the way, and herds of goats, jogging up the hills, bleated like rusty flutes. The carriage spun through a village square – there was no electricity and in the cafes the tricky light of candles and kerosene lamps smoked the faces of masculine company. Two children chased after us into the darkness beyond the village. They clung panting to the carriage as we began a steep careening climb, and our horses, nearing the crest, breathed back on the chilled air a stream of mist. The driver flicked his whip, the horses swayed, the children pointed: look. It was there, Forio, distant, moon-white, the sea shimmering at its edges, a faint sound of vesper bells rising off it like a whirl of birds. *Multo bella?* said the driver. *Multo bella?* said the children.

From *A Capote Reader*, TRUMAN CAPOTE

FIRE

To burn always with this hard, gemlike flame,
to maintain this ecstasy, is success in life.

WALTER PATER

'The sun does not move' (*il sole no si muove*).

Water falls in rain; the earth absorbs it from necessity of moisture; and the sun raises it up not from necessity but by its power.

Flame has its beginning and end in smoke.
The smoke out of which the flame is produced is of much greater heat than the smoke in which this flame ends, because in the first smoke there is the nascent power of the flame, and the last is the dying away of the same flame.

The fire, when heating the water placed in the cooking-pot, says to the water that it does not deserve to stand above the fire, the king of the elements.

The water on finding itself in the proud sea, its element, was seized with a desire to rise above the air; and aided by the element of fire having mounted up in thin vapour, it seemed almost as thin as the air itself; and it fell from the sky, and was then drunk up by the parched earth, where for a long time it lay imprisoned and did penance for its sins.

From *The Notebooks of Leonardo da Vinci*

In the fall the war was always there, but we did not go to it any more. It was cold in the fall in Milan and the dark came very early. Then the electric lights came on, and it was pleasant along the streets looking in the windows. There was much game hanging outside the shops, and snow powdered the fur of the foxes and the wind blew their tails. The deer hung stiff and heavy and empty, and small birds flew in the wind and the wind turned their feathers. It was a cold fall and the wind came down from the mountains.

We were all at the hospital every afternoon, and there were different ways of walking across the town through the dusk to the hospital. Two of the ways were alongside canals, but they were long. Always, though, you crossed a bridge across a canal to enter the hospital. There was a choice of three bridges. On one of them a woman sold roasted chestnuts. It was warm, standing in front of her charcoal fire, and the chestnuts were warm afterward in your pocket. The hospital was very old and very beautiful, and you entered through a gate and walked across a courtyard and out a gate on the other side. There were usually funerals starting from the courtyard. Beyond the old hospital were the new brick pavilions and there we met every afternoon and were all very polite and interested in what was the matter, and sat in the machines that were to make so much difference.

The doctor came up to the machine where I was sitting and said: 'What did you like best to do before the war? Did you practise a sport?'

I said, 'Yes, football.'

'Good,' he said. 'You will be able to play football again better than ever.'

My knee did not bend; the leg dropped straight from the knee to the ankle without a calf, and the machine was to bend the knee and make it move as in riding a tricycle. But it did not bend yet, and instead the machine lurched when it came to the bending part. The doctor said: 'That will all pass. you are a fortunate young man. You will play football again like a champion.'

In the next machine was a major who had a little hand like a baby's. He winked at me when the doctor examined his hand, which was between two leather straps that bounced up and down, and flapped the stiff fingers, and said, 'And will I too play football, captain-doctor?' He had been a very great fencer and, before the war, the greatest fencer in Italy.

The doctor went to his office in a back room and brought a photograph which showed a hand that had been withered almost as small as the major's, before it had taken a machine course, and after was a little larger. The major held the photograph with his good hand and looked at it very carefully. 'A wound?' he asked.

'An industrial accident,' the doctor said.

'Very interesting, very interesting,' the major said, and handed it back to the doctor.

'You have confidence?'

'No,' said the major.

There were three boys who came each day who were about the same age I was. They were all three from Milan, and one of them was to be a lawyer, and one was to be a painter, and one had intended to be a soldier, and after we were finished with the machines, sometimes we walked back together to the Café Cova, which was next door to the Scala. We walked the short way through the communist quarter because we were four together. The people hated us because we were officers, and from a wine-shop someone called out, *A basso gli ufficiali!* as we passed. Another boy, who walked with us sometimes and made us five, wore a black silk handkerchief across his face because he had no nose then and his face was to be rebuilt. He had gone out to the front from the military academy and been wounded within an hour after he had gone into the front line for the first time. They rebuilt his face, but he came from a very old family and they could never get the nose exactly right.

We all had the same medals, except the boy with the black silk bandage across his face, and he had not been at the front long enough to get any medals. The tall boy with a very pale face who was to be a lawyer had been a lieutenant of Arditi and had three medals of the sort we each had only one of. He had lived a very long time with death and was a little detached. We were all a little detached, and there was nothing that held us together except that we met every afternoon at the hospital. Although, as we walked to the Cova through the tough part of town, walking in the dark, with light and singing coming out of the wine-shops, and sometimes having to walk into the street when the men and women would crowd together on the sidewalk so that we would have to jostle them to get by, we felt held together by there being something that had happened that they, the people who disliked us, did not understand.

We ourselves all understood the Cova, where it was rich and warm and not too brightly lighted, and noisy and smoky at certain hours, and there were always girls at the tables and the illustrated papers on a rack on the wall. The girls at the Cova were very patriotic, and I found that the most patriotic people in Italy were the café girls – and I believe they are still patriotic.

The boys at first were very polite about my medals and asked me what I had done to get them. I showed them papers, which were written in very beautiful language and full of *fratellanza* and *abnegazione*, but which really said, with the adjectives removed, that I had been given the medals because I was an American. After that their manner changed a little towards me, although I was their friend against outsiders. I was a friend, but I was never really one of them after they had read the citations, because it had been different with them and they had done very different things to get their medals. I had been wounded, it was true; but we all knew that being wounded, after all, was really an accident. I was never ashamed of the ribbons, though, and sometimes, after the cocktail hour, I would imagine myself having done all the things they had done to get their medals; but walking home at night through the empty streets with the cold wind and all the shops closed, trying to keep near the street lights, I knew that I would never have done such things, and I was very much afraid to die, and often lay in bed at night by myself, afraid to die and wondering how I would be when I went back to the front again.

The three with the medals were like hunting-hawks; and I was not a hawk, although I might seem a hawk to those who had never hunted; they, the three, knew better and so we drifted apart. But I stayed good friends with the boy who had been wounded his first day at the front, because he would never know how he would have turned out; so he could never be accepted either, and I liked him because I thought perhaps he would not have turned out to be a hawk either.

The major, who had been the great fencer, did not believe in bravery, and spent much time while we sat in the machines correcting my grammar. He had complimented me on how I spoke Italian, and we talked together very easily. One day I had said that Italian seemed such an easy language to me that I could not take a great interest in it; everything was so easy to say. 'Ah, yes,' the major said. 'Why, then, do you not take up the use of grammar?' So we took up the use of grammar, and soon Italian was such a difficult language that I was afraid to talk to him until I had the grammar straight in my mind.

'What will you do when the war is over, if it is over?' he asked me. 'Speak grammatically!'

'I will go to the States.'

'Are you married?'

'No, but I hope to be.'

'The more of a fool you are,' he said. He seemed very angry. 'A man must not marry.'

'Why, Signor Maggiore?'

'Don't call me "Signor Maggiore".'

'Why must not a man marry?'

'He cannot marry. He cannot marry,' he said angrily. 'If he is to lose everything, he should not place himself in a position to lose that. He should not place himself in a position to lose. He should find things he cannot lose.'

He spoke very angrily and bitterly, and looked straight ahead while he talked.

'But why should he necessarily lose it?'

'He'll lose it,' the major said. He was looking at the wall. Then he looked down at the machine and jerked his little hand out from between the straps and slapped it hard against his thigh. 'He'll lose it,' he almost shouted. 'Don't argue with me!' then he called to the attendant who ran the machines. 'Come and turn this damned thing off.'

He went back into the other room for the light treatment and the massage. Then I heard him ask the doctor if he might use his telephone and he shut the door. When he came back into the room, I was sitting in another machine. He was wearing his cape and had his cap on, and he came directly towards my machine and put his arm on my shoulder.

'I am so sorry,' he said, and patted me on the shoulder with his good hand. 'I would not be rude. My wife has just died. You must forgive me.'

'Oh –' I said, feeling sick for him. 'I am so sorry.'

He stood there biting his lower lip. 'It is very difficult,' he said. 'I cannot resign myself.'

He looked straight past me and out through the window. Then he began to cry. 'I am utterly unable to resign myself,' he said and choked.

And then crying, his head up looking at nothing, carrying himself straight and soldierly, with tears on both his cheeks and biting his lips, he walked past the machines and out of the door.

From *Men Without Women,* ERNEST HEMINGWAY

THE STORY OF SAN MICHELE

One day I was greatly surprised to receive a visit from old Doctor Pilkington who had very particular reasons for hating me. He said that he and his colleagues had so far waited in vain for my calling on them according to the unwritten rules of etiquette. Since the mountain had not come to Mahomet, Mahomet had come to the mountain. He had nothing in common with Mahomet except his long, white, venerable beard, he looked more like a false prophet than a real one. He said he had come in his quality of the doyen of the resident foreign doctors in Rome to invite me to become a member of their recently formed Society for Mutual Protection with the object of putting an end to the war that had been raging amongst them for so long. All his colleagues had become members except that old ruffian Doctor Campbell with whom none of them were on speaking terms. The thorny question of their professional fees had already been settled to everybody's satisfaction by a mutual agreement fixing the minimum fee at twenty francs, maximum fee at the discretion of each member according to circumstances. No embalmment of man, woman or child was to be made for less than five thousand francs. He was sorry to have to tell me that the Society had of late received several complaints of gross carelessness on my part in collecting my fees and even for not having collected any fees at all. Not later than yesterday Signor Cornacchia, the undertaker, had confided to him almost with tears in his eyes that I had embalmed the wife of the Swedish parson for a hundred lire, a most deplorable breach of loyalty to all my colleagues. He felt sure I would realize the advantage to myself of my becoming a member of their Society for Mutual Protection and would be glad to welcome me amongst them at their next meeting to-morrow.

I answered I was sorry I could not see the advantage either for me or for them of my becoming a member, that anyhow I was willing to discuss with them the fixing of a maximum fee but not of a minimum fee. As to the injections of sublimate they called embalmment, its cost did not exceed fifty francs. Adding another fifty for the loss of time, the sum I had charged for embalming the parson's wife was correct. I intended to earn from the living, not from the dead. I was a doctor, not a hyaena.

He rose from his seat at the word hyaena with a request not to disturb myself in case I ever wished to call him in consultation, he was not available.

I said it was a blow both to myself and to my patients, but that we would have to try to do without him.

I was sorry I had lost my temper, and I told him so at our next meeting, this time in his own house in Via Quattro Fontane. Poor Doctor Pilkington had had a slight stroke the very day after our interview and had sent for me to attend him. He told me the Society for Mutual Protection had broken down, they were all at daggers drawn again, he felt safer in my hands than in theirs. Luckily there was no cause for alarm, in fact I thought he looked livelier after his stroke than before. I tried to cheer him up as well as I could, said there was nothing to worry about and that I had always believed he had already had several slight strokes before. He was soon on his legs again, more active than ever, he was still flourishing when I left Rome.

Soon afterwards I made the acquaintance of his deadly enemy Doctor Campbell, whom he had called an old ruffian. Judging from my first impression he seemed to have hit upon the right diagnosis this time. A more savage-looking old gentleman I never saw, wild blood-shot eyes and cruel lips, the flushed face of a drunkard, all covered with hair like a monkey, and a long, unkempt beard. He was said to be over eighty, the retired old English chemist told me he looked exactly the same thirty years ago when he first arrived in Rome. Nobody knew from where he came, it was rumoured he had been a surgeon in the southern army in the American war. Surgery was his speciality, he was in fact the only surgeon among the foreign doctors, he was on speaking terms with none of them. One day I found him standing by my carriage patting Tappio.

'I envy you that dog,' he said abruptly in a rough voice. 'Do you like monkeys?'

I said I loved monkeys.

He said I was his man, he begged me to come and have a look at his monkey who had been scalded almost to death by upsetting a kettle of boiling water.

We climbed up to his flat at the top of the corner house of Piazza Mignanelli. He begged me to wait in his salon and appeared a minute later with a monkey in his arms, a huge baboon all wrapped up in bandages.

'I am afraid he is very bad,' said the old doctor in quite a different voice, tenderly caressing the emaciated face of his monkey. 'I do not know what I shall do if he dies, he is my only friend. I have brought him up on the bottle since he was a baby, his dear mother died when she gave birth to him. She was almost as big as a gorilla, you never saw such a darling, she was quite human. I do not mind in the least cutting my fellow creatures to pieces, I rather like it, but I have no more courage left in me to dress his scalded little body, he suffers so horribly when I try to disinfect his wounds that I cannot stand it any longer. I am sure you like animals, will you take him in hand?'

We unwrapped the bandages soaked with blood and pus, it was a pitiful sight, his whole body was one terrible wound.

'He knows you are a friend or he would not sit as still as he does, he never allows anybody but me to touch him. He knows everything, he has more brains than all the foreign doctors in Rome put together. He has eaten nothing for four days,' he went on, with a tender expression in his blood-shot eyes. 'Billy, my son, won't you oblige your papa by trying this fig?'

I said I wished we had a banana, there was nothing monkeys liked better.

He said he would telegraph at once to London for a bunch of bananas, never mind the cost.

I said it was a question of keeping up his strength. We poured a little warm milk into his mouth, but he spat it out at once.

'He cannot swallow anymore,' groaned his master, 'I know what it means, he is dying.'

We improvised with a sort of feeding tube and this time he kept the milk to the delight of the old doctor.

Billy got slowly better. I saw him every day for a fortnight, and I ended by becoming quite fond both of him and his master. Soon I found him sitting in his specially constructed rocking-chair on the sunny terrace by the side of his master, a bottle of whisky on the table between them. The old doctor was a great believer in whisky to steady one's hand before an operation. To judge from the number of empty whisky bottles in the corner of the terrace, his surgical practice must have been considerable. Alas! they were both addicted to drink. I had often caught Billy helping himself to a little whisky and soda out of his master's glass. The doctor had told me whisky was the best possible tonic for monkeys, it had saved the life of Billy's beloved mother after her pneumonia. One evening I came upon them on their terrace, both blind drunk. Billy was executing a sort of negro dance on the table round the whisky bottle, the old doctor sat leaning back in his chair clapping his hands to mark the time, singing in a hoarse voice:

'Billy, my son, Billy, my sonny, soooooooonny!' They neither heard nor saw me coming. I stared in consternation at the happy family. The face of the intoxicated monkey had become quite human, the face of the old drunkard looked exactly like the face of a gigantic gorilla. The family likeness was unmistakable.

'Billy, my son, Billy, my son, soooooooony!'

Was it possible? No, of course it was not possible but it made me feel quite creepy . . .

AXEL MUNTHE

GARIBALDI'S DEFENCE OF THE ROMAN REPUBLIC

And still, over the plains and mountain roads of Italy, the Austrians in their white coats and shakos moved unceasingly on their fruitless, mechanical task of repression; stared at with a vague but growing antipathy by the common people, with horror by Shelley, and with disgust by Byron.

'Men,' Garibaldi declared, are reformed 'by example more than by doctrine.' And so his doctrine was of one word – *Avanti!*

Italian artists, almost to a man, enlisted during the days that followed his arrival, if they had not done so before, either in his own Legion, or in the Civic Guard, or in the special Students' Corps, which consisted of three hundred University men and artists.

One of the Italians in after years told the story of his conversion to the Rev. H.R. Haweis. He had come out, he said, with his artist friends, to see what was going on, one day, when Garibaldi was recruiting in a public place in Rome.

'I had no idea (he told the English clergyman) of enlisting. I was a young artist; I only went out of curiosity – but oh! I

197

shall never forget that day when I saw him on his beautiful white horse in the market-place, with his noble aspect, his calm, kind face, his high, smooth forehead, his light hair and beard. Every one said the same. He reminded us of nothing so much as of our Saviour's head in the galleries. I could not resist him. I left my studio. I went after him; we could not help it.'

It was no passing emotion of youth, for eleven years afterwards the narrator was fighting for Garibaldi in Naples.

Many of the Neapolitan soldiers had, in fact, again been scared by the 'red devil,' whom they declared to be bullet-proof; the giant black man behind him was Beelzebub, his father. In plaintive mutiny some cried out to their King: 'You are going to Naples, and we to the slaughter.'

– Roma, o Morte! –

'We sat down on the ground in the square; and, when the terrified inhabitants observed from the surrounding heights this admirable spirit of order and self-restraint, they hurried down to welcome us, threw open their houses and shops, and in a few minutes the whole village had regained its accustomed activity. They then related to us how many superstitious fables the Neapolitans had spread among them; according to which we were so many ogres let loose by the devil, to devour children and burn down houses; and the fantastic costumes of Garibaldi and his followers had contributed not a little to increase the ignorant fears of the natives.'

How far, under these conditions, Garibaldi would have succeeded in rousing the Kingdom to revolt was never put to the
test; for at this point he was recalled.

Garibaldi had now won Italy's devotion, and was helping to
unite her divided children by their common pride in himself.
Ere long he was to dazzle the imagination of Europe, even of his
enemies; but the chief glory of the Third of June does not
belong to Garibaldi, but to the slain – the seed that had fallen
into the ground and died, and was to bring forth fruit in its
season.

Finally, when the ammunition was running low, Garibaldi
headed a last desperate charge of his own Legionaries and some
of Pasi's line regiment against the French positions. Again, as on
the night before, it was cold steel, and again Garibaldi fought in
the front, dealing death with his sword, reckless of his life, and
against all the chances remaining unscathed. The French could
not be dislodged; gradually the firing slackened. A truce was
arranged at mid-day for the gathering of the dead and
wounded, and Garibaldi was summoned to the Capitol, where
the Assembly was discussing the question of surrender.
Although the ruins of the Spada had not been stormed, all
knew that Rome had fallen.

To starve in the slums of foreign cities, or serve far off under a
hated flag, while the country for which a man's best friends
have died has fallen back into servitude, perhaps for ever, may
appear a romantic fate in the retrospect, after Italy has been
redeemed, but to the actual sufferers it was bitter as the lot of
Andromache.

Garibaldi brushed aside the idea of continuing the defence of Rome. As to surrender, he does not seem to have discussed it. There remained the third plan – to carry the Government and army into the wilderness. This he approved. *Dovunque saremo, colà sarà Roma.* ('Wherever we go, there will be Rome'), he said.

'Fortune, who betrays us to-day, will smile on us to-morrow. I am going out from Rome. Let those who wish to continue the war against the stranger, come with me. I offer neither pay, nor quarters, nor provisions; I offer hunger, thirst, forced marches, battles and death. Let him who loves his country in his heart and not with his lips only, follow me.'

G.M. TREVELYAN

THE MAFIA

Historians generally agree that the authentic Mafia got its start with Mazzini's flamboyant ally Giuseppe Garibaldi. It was Garibaldi who drove out the last of the Bourbon kings and united Sicily to the new Italian state. Sicilians flocked to join him in an explosion of joyous excitement when his Red Shirts landed in Palermo in 1860. About two thousand *picciotti* were among them, bold young peasants, half-brigand, half-rebel, who used to hide in caves of tufa stone called *maha* in Arabic. That is probably where 'Mafia' comes from; Garibaldi's *picciotti* were spoken of as *squadri della mafia*.

They were dazzled by Garibaldi's promises of dignity and

social justice. Sicily was prostrate after two millennia of foreign rule – humiliated, eaten with corruption, destitute – but the young Italian nation failed to redeem it. The promises were broken, the Sicilians forgotten. In the absence of a state, the *picciotti* banded together and took over.

There is no document stating that this band was the Mafia. Nevertheless, an official dispatch dated 1865 cites it by name for the first time as a virulent, criminal secret society.

Made members of the Mafia in Sicily constitute only a fraction of one percent of the island's population. Those who support them knowingly and willingly are a small minority. Millions of honest Sicilians suffer the Mafia only because they have been terrorized into silence. The bravest and most gallant men and women who have ever fought the Mafia have been the Sicilians themselves.

CLAIRE STERLING

Two Sicilian magistrates, Giovanni Falcone and Paolo Borsellino, took the war against the mafia further than anyone had dared before. That war, which would ultimately claim their lives, went on to topple the ruling coalition that had governed Italy since World War II. The engineers of the renowned 'maxi-trials', Falcone and Borsellino succeeded in penetrating the mafia's code of silence and revealing, for the first time, the inner structure of Sicily's Cosa Nostra. By winning the cooperation of Tommaso Buscetta – the first of many Sicilian bosses to become witnesses – they revolutionized organized crime prosecutions in the United States as well as in Italy. 'Before Buscetta we didn't even know the mafia's real name,' the prosecutors said.

In 1876, a young member of parliament from Tuscany, Leopoldo Franchetti, traveled to Sicily to report on the strange island that had quickly become the most troubled and recalcitrant part of the newly united Italian state. Franchetti was enchanted by the beauty of Palermo, the majesty of the baroque palaces, the exquisite courtesy and hospitality of the people, the languorous, sunny weather, the exotic palm trees and the intoxicating perfume of the orange and lemon blossoms of the Conca d'Oro's fertile citrus groves.

> Someone who had just arrived might well believe . . . that
> Sicily was the easiest and most pleasant place in the entire
> world. But if [the traveler] stays a while, begins to read the
> newspapers and listens carefully (he wrote), bit by bit
> everything changes around him . . . He hears that the
> guard of that orchard was killed with a rifle shot coming
> from behind that wall because the owner hired him rather
> than someone else . . . Just over there, an owner who
> wanted to rent his groves as he saw fit heard a bullet
> whistle past his head in friendly warning and afterwards
> gave in. Elsewhere, a young man who had dedicated
> himself to setting up nursery schools in the outskirts of
> Palermo was shot at . . . because certain people who
> dominate the common people in that area, feared that, by
> benefiting the poorer classes, he would acquire some of the
> influence on the population that they wanted to reserve

exclusively for themselves. The violence and the murders take the strangest forms . . . There is a story about a former priest, who became the crime leader in a town near Palermo and administered the last rites to some of his own victims. After a certain number of these stories, the perfume of orange and lemon blossoms starts to smell of corpses.

Sicily is a place where almost nothing is what it seems.

Survivors of twenty-five hundred years of foreign invasions and of countless violent and corrupt rulers, Sicilians are a skeptical people. When I asked a Sicilian friend why he didn't trust a local politician with a reputation as an outspoken anti-mafia crusader, he replied: 'He's alive, isn't he? If he'd really done anything against the mafia, he'd already be dead.'

Death is the only certain truth.

The moment of truth came for Judge Giovanni Falcone on May 23, 1992, when he, his wife, and three bodyguards were killed by a massive explosion that ripped apart the highway leading from the airport at Punta Raisi to Palermo.

It came just two months later, on July 19, for Falcone's close friend and fellow prosecutor, Paolo Borsellino, and five bodyguards – blown up as Borsellino arrived for a Sunday visit with his mother in downtown Palermo.

The day before Dalla Chiesa was killed, he spoke with Ralph Jones, the American consul in Palermo, expressing his frustrations and appealing to the U.S. government to pressure Rome into granting him the powers he had sought unsuccessfully for three months. He told Jones a story from his experience during the 1970s as a colonel in charge of the *carabinieri* unit in Palermo. 'One day he received a phone call from the captain of the *carabinieri* for the town of Palma di Montechiaro who told him he had been threatened by the local mafia boss,' Jones explained later. 'Dalla Chiesa left immediately for Palma di Montechiaro, arriving in the late afternoon. He took the captain by the arm and began walking with him slowly up and down the main street. Everyone looked at them. In the end, this odd couple stopped in front of the house of the local mafia boss. The two stayed long enough to make clear to everyone that the captain was not alone. "All I am asking is that someone take me by the arm and walk with me," the general said. A few hours later he was killed.'

Buscetta was the first 'made man' to talk, the first *pentito*.

At the beginning, Buscetta wanted to put Falcone on notice. 'I trust you, Judge Falcone, and I trust deputy police chief Gianni De Gennaro. But I don't trust anyone else. I don't believe the Italian state has the real intention of fighting the mafia . . . I want to warn you, Judge. After this interrogation you will become a celebrity. But they will try to destroy you physically and professionally. And they will do the same to me. Never forget that you are opening an account with Cosa Nostra that will only be settled when you die. Are you sure you want to go ahead with this?'

That day, Buscetta, still recovering from his near fatal suicide attempt, limited himself to making a brief statement. 'I want to make clear that I am not a stool pigeon . . . I am not a "penitent," in that my revelations are not motivated by base calculations of personal interest. I have spent my life as a *mafioso* and I have made mistakes, for which I am prepared to pay the consequences, without asking for sentence reductions or special treatment. In the interest of society, of my children and other young people, I intend to reveal all that I know about the cancer of the mafia, so that future generations can live in a more human and dignified way.' Then, sick and exhausted, he asked to return to his cell to rest. Falcone did not press him to continue.

This was the first of an extraordinary series of sessions that would last for the rest of the summer, that would radically alter Falcone's understanding of the Sicilian mafia. Buscetta started their second session like a professor beginning an introductory course. 'The word "mafia" is a literary creation, while the real *mafiosi* call themselves simply "men of honor" . . . and the organization as a whole is called Cosa Nostra.'

As he fingered the killers in the great mafia war and revealed the names of those who had ordered the assassination of Palermo's 'excellent cadavers,' Buscetta insisted that, while his information was often secondhand, it was as rock solid as if he had witnessed the events himself because 'men of honor' had an absolute obligation to tell the truth to other men of honour when talking about mafia business. The revelations of Stefano Bontate, Salvatore Inzerillo, Gaetano Badalamenti and Antonio Salamone 'have the value of absolute truth,' Buscetta insisted. 'I realize that I am expressing a concept that is hard for anyone who is not Sicilian or who is not a *mafioso* to grasp . . . A man of honor . . . must always tell the truth. Whoever breaks this rule, since he has the right not to speak, is guilty of a serious violation that is punishable even with death.'

While many might have laughed at the notion of an obligation to always tell the truth within an organization where killing, stealing and cheating are the order of the day, Falcone had the wisdom to listen to Buscetta carefully. Clearly the current generation of Cosa Nostra had made a mockery of its 'code of honor.' The elaborate laws regulating members' behaviour were an important source of internal strength that gave the mafia enormous advantages over other forms of organized crime and helped it to survive for 120 years. Men of honor were extremely disciplined criminals, who generally avoided gratuitous violence, often went to extreme lengths to protect their own kind, and never cooperated with police – all of which had made them extremely difficult to prosecute. '[The mafia] expresses a subculture which is the criminal extreme of certain values that, by themselves, are not bad: courage, friendship, respect for tradition,' Falcone said in a 1986 interview. Falcone was convinced that until the government took the mafia as seriously as it took itself, efforts to combat it would be doomed to failure. And so, rather than limiting himself to a discussion of specific crimes and criminals. Falcone drew Buscetta out on the more apparently 'folkloristic' elements of mafia life.

'No one will ever find any written codes of the mafia, but its laws are as rigid as iron and are universally accepted,' Buscetta said. 'Similarly, no one will ever find membership lists but the bond that ties men of honor is stronger and more impenetrable than if it were written in any document . . . In my opinion, one of the principal mistakes that has been made in the war against the mafia has been to ignore this reality that every man of honor knows very well.'

The mood of the city, as anticipation of the maxi-trial built, swung back and forth between widespread skepticism and wild euphoria.

For the first time, a genuine anti-mafia culture was developing in Palermo. New civic anti-mafia groups were springing up. The family members of mafia victims formed their own extremely active group, Il Coordinamento Anti-mafia (The Anti-mafia Network). Many local parish priests were speaking out against the mafia in their sermons or trying to create alternatives for young people in the poorest neighborhoods where the mafia did most of its recruiting.

'The people are beginning to root for us,' Paolo Borsellino told Falcone as he felt the mood of the city change. Falcone, imbued with a deep Sicilian pessimism, was not so sure: 'They're standing at the window, waiting to see who wins the bullfight.'

As Buscetta had predicted, Falcone had become a celebrity, the symbol of the war against the mafia, his picture regularly in the national newspapers. His reserved, Sicilian manner – with his dark beard and dark eyes – had taken on a legendary aura.

'I am a dead man,' Falcone said. He was acutely aware of the dangers of political isolation in the war on the mafia, recalling what General Dalla Chiesa had said shortly before his death: 'I've understood the new rules of the game: they kill the man in power when this fatal combination has come about: he has become too dangerous but he can be killed because he is isolated.' The victory in the maxi-trial had proved again how dangerous Falcone was, while the rejection that came on its heels showed how deeply isolated he was. 'I'm a dead man,' he repeated.

November 1990, in the small Sicilian city of Gela, eight people were killed and seven others were wounded in four different mafia hits in the space of a twenty-five-minute period. War between local clans had claimed more than 100 lives in Gela during the previous three years – an impressive total for a town of only 90,000 inhabitants.

'I am like a bear in a cage,' Falcone told his old boss Antonino Caponetto. In late 1990, Falcone began recording his frustrations in a diary, recalling Rocco Chinnici's words of warning: 'Keep a diary, you never know.'

1991. When a journalist from the Rome daily paper *La Repubblica* went to visit Falcone on Tuesday, May 19, Falcone appeared discouraged by the continued paralysis of the Italian political system. 'Cosa Nostra never forgets,' he said. 'The enemy is always there, ready to strike . . . This is why we must act quickly to build the super-prosecutor's office . . . But we are not even able to agree on the election of the president of the Republic.'

At the end of the week, on Saturday, May 23, the leaders of the major parties were still meeting to try to unblock the political log-jam. After doing a morning's work, Giovanni Falcone left Rome for Palermo, where he returned every weekend. His wife, Francesca, had remained in her job in Sicily, although she was scheduled to be transferred to join Falcone in Rome. That particular week, Francesca had business in Rome and Falcone, rather than leave on Friday evening, postponed his departure until Saturday afternoon so that they could travel together. They left from the Ciampino military airport outside Rome, in a government plane that took off at 4:40 and touched down at Punta Raisi airport in Palermo just over an hour later. A three-car police motorcade with seven bodyguards met them on their arrival. But, since security measures had been cut back in recent years, no helicopter surveyed the route to the city in anticipation of Falcone's arrival. As a result, no one noticed the unusual amount of activity that had taken place earlier in the day next to the highway near the town of Capaci just a few kilometers from the airport. A team of 'men of honor,' dressed as construction workers, had put the finishing touches on the huge, 500-kilo stash of plastic explosives they had placed in a large metal drain pipe that passed underneath the highway. As evening approached, a group of men clustered around a small shack a hundred yards back from the roadside where a remote-control detonator was hidden, scanning the traffic moving from the airport toward the city.

In a minor breach of standard security procedures, Giovanni Falcone took the wheel of his bulletproof Fiat Croma, a small gesture of freedom in a highly restricted life. Francesca got in beside him in the front seat, while their driver, Giuseppe Constanze, moved to the back seat. As the motorcade drove past Capaci, the entire highway was ripped open by a massive explosion that seemed like the epicenter of an earthquake. All three cars were swallowed up, bent and twisted by the blast that created a huge crater and tore up a quarter of mile of road. 'All hell seemed to open up before us in a second,' said an eye-witness whose car was directly behind the motorcade. 'A terrifying explosion . . . a scene from the apocalypse, screams of terror and then an unreal silence . . .'

If Falcone had not insisted on driving, he might have lived. He was fifty-three years old.

The Italian parliament called for a day of mourning and suspended its session until after Falcone's funeral on Monday. In Sicily a general strike was proclaimed, shutting all stores and business for a day. The closed coffins of the five victims of the Capaci bombing were laid out the next day in the huge, cavernous marble lobby of the Palermo Palace of Justice, the scene of Falcone's greatest triumphs and bitterest defeats, the place that Falcone had left in disgust just over a year before. Besides the friends and colleagues of the victims, some were surprised to see thousands of ordinary Palermitans, men and women from the silent majority of that city that, as Falcone had said several years earlier, were 'waiting at the window to see who would win the bullfight.'

Across the city, a new phenomenon sprang up: people started hanging bedsheets out of their windows with slogans of protest or grief written across them: 'Palermo demands Justice . . .' 'Get the *mafiosi* out of government!' 'Falcone, you remain in our hearts.'

The funeral of Falcone was a national drama, broadcast live on national television. People wept at the impassioned pleas of Rosaria Schifani, the twenty-three-year-old widow of slain bodyguard Vito Schifani, who cried out, 'Men of the mafia, I will forgive you, but you must get down on your knees!'

Many commentators saw the assassination of Falcone as symbolic of the death of the Italian state. 'Falcone should have been protected better than any other person in our country, because no one more than he embodied the state,' wrote Claudio Magris in *Corriere della Sera*. 'The fact that we have been unable or unwilling to protect him means that the state does not exist.'

One of Italy's leading philosophers, Norberto Bobbio, declared that the death of Falcone 'made me ashamed to be Italian.'

As the Italian public began to realize how much they had lost in Falcone, the media shifted the tremendous weight of its attention onto Borsellino. As Falcone was beatified as a martyr, Borsellino was hailed as the new redeemer – a dangerous amplification of the fight against the mafia that drew all eyes to Borsellino.

Agnese Borsellino could tell something was upsetting her husband when he returned home on Saturday, July 18. Finally, after she insisted they go out for a drive, he unburdened himself. Although he did not name names, he said he had heard damning evidence against a police investigator and a prosecutor.

On Sunday, July 19 Borsellino and his six bodyguards drove [back] into Palermo to see the prosecutor's mother. Cars were parked outside his mother's apartment in Via D'Amelio when Borsellino's three-car escort arrived just after five that afternoon. Several days earlier, his security details had asked that a 'no parking' zone be created in the area to protect against the possibility of car bombs, but the request had not been examined by the committee in charge of government security in Palermo. Borsellino got out of his car, surrounded by five agents – Walter Cusina, Claudio Traina, Vincenzo Li Muli, Agostino Catalano and Emanuela Loi, all of whom held pistols and machine guns. A sixth agent remained at the wheel of the lead car, as he had been trained to do. As Borsellino approached the gate of the apartment building to ring his mother's bell, he and the five bodyguards who surrounded him were blown into the air by an explosion that could be heard miles away across Palermo. Even though there were at least thirty feet between the front gate and the entrance to the building, the blast broke windows all the way up to the eleventh floor. The apartments facing the street on the first four floors were completely gutted.

Rather than shutting the mouths of the mafia witnesses, the assassinations of Falcone and Borsellino seemed to have the opposite effect. With the floodgates finally opened, the police suddenly had more witnesses than they had time in which to question them.

Although there are many people who are trying to restore the old status quo, there are reasons to believe that something important has changed in Sicily in the last ten to fifteen years. The social consensus the mafia once enjoyed has been seriously eroded. 'The mafia is not disappearing, but the people who used to revere us and used to identify with the mafia, now tolerate us because they are afraid,' Leonardo Messina testified before the Italian parliament. 'People in Sicily are beginning to believe in the state because now even the son of a street sweeper or a shoemaker may go to university and no longer wants to be subject to the mafia.' he said.

Falcone and Borsellino had a lot to do with this social change. Past crusaders against the mafia, from Mussolini's 'Iron Prefect' Cesare Mori to General Dalla Chiesa were, like Garibaldi's conquering troops, northern Italians on a mission to civilize the island and link it to the rest of Italy. Falcone and Borsellino offered a new image of the state: serious, uncompromisingly honest and profoundly Sicilian. By bringing the mafia to trial, they proved that the mafia is not invincible. And they did so through the scrupulous use of the legal code. 'The most revolutionary thing you could do in Sicily,' Falcone once said, 'is simply to apply the law and punish the guilty.'

From *Excellent Cadavers: Mafia and the Death of the First Italian Republic*, ALEXANDER STILLE

A Sicilian Tragedy

In January 1968 an earthquake destroyed a number of villages in the poverty-stricken valley of Belice in north-west Sicily. Over five hundred people were killed and 90,000 rendered homeless. The President of the Republic, Giuseppe Saragat, immediately promised that the government 'will do everything possible to aid the people made homeless by the earthquake'. Vast sums of money were assigned by Parliament for the reconstruction of the Belice villages. Nine years later, 60,000 people in the valley were still living in the Nissen huts which had been erected immediately after the earthquake. Huge and surreal infrastructures had been built in the valley – roads that led nowhere, flyovers used only by flocks of sheep, pedestrian walkways with no pedestrians, and so on. Meanwhile, not a single new house had been assigned by the authorities to any of the villagers. The money voted by Parliament had not been spent, or it had been misspent or simply embezzled.

In December, 1975, Don Antonio Riboldi, the parish priest of Santa Ninfa in the Belice, organized the writing of some seven hundred letters by the primary-school children of the Belice to the Senators and Deputies of the Italian Parliament. One of these was from Giovanna Bellafiore to Giulio Andreotti, the veteran Christian Democrat leader. Andreotti replied on 26 February 1976. It is worth reproducing this correspondence as an end-piece to this chapter, not as a personal indictment of Andreotti, but as an example of how the pervasive torpor of the state had triumphed. For a brief moment, for all their failings, the revolutionary groups had challenged this state of affairs from below: organizations like Magistratura Democratica had been small but significant attempts to launch a radical mobilization within the state apparatus. However, the challenge had faltered, leaving the state unreformed and the politicians apologetic but acquiescent.

Santa Ninfa
16 February 1976

Dear Honourable Andreotti Giulio,

My name is Giovanna Bellafiore. I am the little girl who wrote to you before Christmas, but you didn't reply, which is not right.

I live in a prefabricated hut which is 24 metres square and has only one room. The rain comes in and leaks on the bed, on the wardrobe and on the plates which have been put in the rack to dry. Perhaps you didn't reply because the problem is too hot for you to handle. I beg you to intervene on our behalf, something which no deputy has so far done. Often there is no electricity and no running water in our huts. You Members of Parliament have comfortable houses to live in, with central heating, and you certainly couldn't understand the type of life which we *baraccati* have to live, with no space for anything, no room to study or play, or even for the chairs to put round the table. Do you know that when we eat I sit on my Daddy's and Mummy's bed? In fact the table is almost attached to the bed. If you don't believe my letter I invite you to come and sleep and eat in my house for a week.

Why is no one taking an interest in us victims of the earthquake? I beg you not to throw away this letter because I'm still waiting for a reply and I beg you to discuss the matter in Parliament with the other *onorevoli*.

Yours
Giovanna Bellafiore

Giullo Andreotti replied:

Roma
26 February, 1976

Dear Child,
I received your little letter of 16 February . . .

And he sent her a doll. Twenty-two years later, the homeless are still living in Nissen huts.

From *A History of Contemporary Italy*, PAUL GINSBORG

CALVINO'S LAMENT

Back in 1982 Italo Calvino wrote a lament for his country about shared – and therefore diffused – responsibility. Entitled *Apologo Sull'onestà nel Paese dei Corrotti* ('An Apology for Honesty in the Country of Corrupt Men'), it was a savage indictment of the Italian system.

Once upon a time (he wrote) there was a country which was based on illegality. It was not that there was a shortage of laws. Not that the political system was not based on principles which more or less everyone said that they shared. But this system, posited on a large number of centres of power, needed excessive amounts of financing and these means they could only obtain illegally.

At the same time, no centre of power felt in the least guilty about this way of financing its activities. Because in its sense of right and wrong, what was done for the good of the group was legitimate, even desirable, as every group identified its own power with the common good.

From time to time, some magistrate or another would take it upon himself to apply the law. This would cause minor tremors in some centre of power, and even the arrests of people who until then had regarded themselves as protected, unpunishable. In these cases the widespread feeling, besides that of satisfaction that justice had been done, was the suspicion that in fact we were dealing with a settling of accounts between one centre of power and another.

There are millions of Italians who for years have been clamouring for justice and fairness in public life and who see the removal of a whole political class as a sign of the strength of their peculiar form of democracy, that same democracy which brought them to this sorry pass.

From *The New Italians*, CHARLES RICHARDS

FAMILY MATTERS

Family in Italy means much more than grown-up children taking round their tray of cakes, freshly purchased and specially wrapped, to the parental home for Sunday lunch or major holidays. The family represents more than the great occasions, the weddings and the christenings and the first communions, which are celebrated with such evident gusto. Family provides the network of the deepest and most important relationships of Italian society. Now the same could be said of most other societies, but in Italy the family has a hold on loyalty which is so strong, so tenacious, so resistant to the evolution of other norms of behaviour that it can still rightly be called the basic building block of society . . .

The size of the family may have changed enormously, but the ties have not. The most stable relationship of all in Italy remains [that] between mother and son. From the moment a blue ribbon is tied on to the outside of the front door to signify a male birth, a son is the pampered centre of attention. *Mammismo* has none of the connotations of 'mother's boy' in English-speaking countries. It merely means that sons are spoiled by their mothers, which they almost always are. It is such a stereotype of Italian life, but little has changed. 'Men exchange one mother for another when they marry,' the writer Dacia Maraini asserted. Even in the 1990s, few men leave home until they marry. One often meets single men in their thirties who still live with their mothers. In Anglo-Saxon countries young people generally go to university away from their home towns to cut the apron strings. In Italy there is scarcely any provision for student lodging. Most young people simply cannot afford to leave home and tend to go to the local university.

The strength of the mother-son relationship can greatly prejudice the successful fulfilment of subsequent relationships. The model of the Madonna and Child is *the* stereotypic Italian relationship. Time and again, when sons sin, in their mothers' eyes they can do no wrong.

Italian men appear to be quite at ease in the presence of women. Their legendary charm, their ability to flatter and their appreciation of attractive women have all reinforced the myth that they are wonderful lovers. Sexual prowess and the Latin lover are, of course, fundamental to the image of the Italian male. One senior Italian politician was known as 'The Orgasm'. Yet it seems Italian manhood falls short of the myth. The talents of the Latin Lover have to be learnt, not inherited. In Tapani in Sicily an enterprising businessman set up a school for the Latin lover, to teach techniques evidently not acquired as birthright.

From *The New Italians*, CHARLES RICHARDS

CIRCLES OF HELL

Ever since the victory in North Africa, the British Foreign Office and American State Department had been collaborating on the drafting of a surrender document. The project was not going well and there were major differences, with the British demanding much harsher conditions than the Americans considered necessary. News of Mussolini's fall was received in London on 26 July and the Prime Minister lost no time in writing Roosevelt on the possible opportunities it presented:

> Changes announced in Italy probably portend peace
> proposals. Let us consult together so as to take joint action.
> The present stage may only be transition. But anyhow
> Hitler will feel very lonely when Mussolini is down and
> out. No one can be quite sure this may not go further.

Roosevelt had already heard the news and penned his own thoughts. Their telegrams crossed:

The news from Rome came, but this time it seems to be true. If any overtures come we must be certain of the use of all Italian territory and transportation against the Germans in the north and against the whole Balkan Peninsula, as well as the use of airfields of all kinds . . . It is my thought that we should come as close as possible to unconditional surrender followed by good treatment of the Italian populace. But I think also that the head Devil should be surrendered together with his chief partners in crime. In no event should our officers in the field fix on any general terms without your approval and mine. Let me have your thoughts.

Even while the two leaders were exchanging thoughts Eisenhower acted. On 17 July he made a broadcast to the Italian people which had been vetted by Murphy and Harold Macmillan, his political advisers.

We commend the Italian people on ridding themselves of Mussolini, the man who involved them in war as the tool of Hitler and brought them to the verge of disaster. The greatest obstacle which divided the Italian people from the United Nations has been removed by the Italians themselves. The only remaining obstacle on the road to honourable peace is the German aggressor who is still on Italian soil. You want peace. You can have it immediately. We are coming to you as Liberators. Your part is to cease immediately any assistance to the German Military Forces in your country. If you do this we will rid you of the

Germans and deliver you from the horrors of war. As you have already seen in Sicily our occupation will be mild and beneficial. Your men will return to their normal life and to their productive avocations and, provided all British and Allied prisoners now in your hands are restored safely to us and not taken away to Germany, the hundreds of thousands of Italian prisoners captured by us in Tunisia and Sicily will return to the countless Italian homes who long for them. The ancient liberties and traditions of your country will be restored.

The Allied leaders indulged in much wild speculation – the Italians would allow the Germans to leave, or would prevent them from leaving or, indeed, the Germans would choose to leave. Churchill got tetchy with Eisenhower for assuming that an overture would come to him, for the Italians might just as easily make an approach via the Vatican, Switzerland or Portugal. Anthony Eden got upset with Cordell Hull at the State Department and Churchill became angry with Eden for being too finicky over the legality of an Italian armistice. All of this occurred before the Italians had even made an approach.

Amid all of this only one man gave any thought to what the Germans might have in mind – George Marshall: 'In this very connection it must be remembered that in North Africa a relatively small German garrison had produced a serious factor of delay to our operations. A German decision to support Italy might make intended operations extremely difficult and time consuming.' It is quite astonishing, but in all the official documents and papers which are now available, as well as the memoirs and biographies of the notables, there is no other reference at this time to any consideration of the fighting qualities of the Germans.

Flights into the realms of fantasy continued until 4 August when Churchill left on the *Queen Mary* for the Quadrant Conference at Quebec. The Italian surrender seduced the British into producing strong arguments to support a limited operation on the Italian mainland and the Americans succumbed to British pressure.

Meanwhile Badoglio was assuring the Germans that nothing had changed. Thus on the day he was appointed he made the following proclamation to the Italian people:

Italians! By order of His Majesty the King Emperor, I today assume the military government of the country with full powers. The war goes on. Italy, hit hard in her invaded provinces, in her destroyed cities, maintains her given word, a jealous guardian of her thousand-year tradition. Let the ranks be serried around His Majesty the King Emperor, a living image of the Fatherland, an example for all. The order I have received is clear and precise and it will be carried out scrupulously and whoever cherishes illusions of being able to disrupt normal development or trying to disturb public order, will be inexorably punished.

Long live Italy, Long live the King.
Signed, Marshal of Italy Pietro Badoglio
Rome: July 15th, 1943

The announcement, which was published in numerous London newspapers and armed newspapers in the Mediterranean, was also accompanied by columns of speculation about when the Allies would invade mainland Italy. So what happened subsequently could hardly have come as a surprise to the Germans.

The Italian people and the Germans were united in the response to Badoglio's proclamation. No-one believed a word of it.

> Why should we crawl up the leg like a harvest-bug from
> the ankle upwards? Let us rather strike at the knees.
>
> WINSTON CHURCHILL, August 1943

Even though the armistice had been signed it had no meaning until it could be made public. In the intervening period the Allies continued to kill Italians. Three days after the signing of the armistice, one of the heaviest air raids of the war to date was launched against Frascati. Situated about 20 miles south-east of Rome, Frascati was a legitimate military target by virtue of numerous German military headquarters and staffs. But the Allied bombers, with their usual degree of imprecision, managed to cause slight damage to one such installation and kill hundreds of women and children in the process.

There had been the usual witch-hunts in towns and villages, providing an opportunity to settle old scores and pursue family feuds and vendettas.

There was an embryo Ministry of Foreign Affairs at Brindisi with a handful of secretaries and clerks; it received no diplomatic recognition.

The Roman Catholic Church remained a symbol for national unity for all Italians, with the exception of the diehard communists. But it was a target for Allied suspicion because of the Pope's perceived pro-fascist policy of appeasement. Pius XII regarded communism as a greater evil than fascism. He refused to sanction or bless Partisan activities in the name of resistance because he believed the movement was communist-dominated; yet he blessed Mussolini's legions as they marched off to war. Pius XII won no friends among the Allies for his criticism of the bombing of the monastery at Monte Cassino, while never condemning the Germans for their atrocities, the execution of innocent civilians, the taking of hostages. There is no evidence to suggest that the Pope was pro-German, only that he saw Hitler to be the least of several evils. Apologists maintain that Pius XII, a consummate diplomat versed in all the subtleties of international politics in the Curia, played the only hand he could, and ensured that the Vatican State survived.

On the plus side, hundreds of Allied soldiers and airmen, trapped behind German lines, found sanctuary in the Vatican. The Pope also sent his nuncio to Berlin to plead with Hitler for the Jews. The interview ended with Hitler smashing a glass at the nuncio's feet.

When the Germans demanded a ransom in gold for Rome's Jews, the Pope ordered a number of priceless artefacts to be melted down. As a member of the wealthy Pacelli family he also spent a considerable amount of his personal fortune to help ransom Jews from Nazi persecution and certain death. Little of this was known at the time, and when the Allies came to liberate Rome the Pope was held in very low esteem by the High

Command. These same generals, however, fell over themselves for an audience when the city was free.

Nardina Donatini was twenty-one years old. She lived with her parents in Marradi, a market town in the Apennines, north of Florence. Monday was market day in Marradi, when the town was always busy. Stalls were set up in the main square and peasants came from the surrounding villages to sell their produce, mostly livestock, clothes, linen and embroidery. Marradi was an important road junction which had two bridges over the River Lamone, one steel for the railway and the other stone for the road. For weeks trainloads of German troops and supplies had passed through Marradi on their way south to the front.

It was a time of sadness in my family, for just two months previously my sister, who was seventeen, had died of meningitis. We didn't know where the Allies were, but we all knew it wouldn't be long before Marradi too would be liberated. There was a small German garrison which came to our town when Mussolini fell from power. Their commandant was really very kind, he had lent his car to take my sister to the hospital in Florence. But many of our young men had been taken away to Germany to work; others had fled into the hills to hide or join the Partisans.

We were always frightened of the SS because they would come into the town to look for our menfolk and take them away; some we never saw again. The SS wore the best uniforms and were handsome men, but very cruel and we always ran away and hid when the SS patrol came to Marradi.

The Americans bombed Marradi on this market day. I was on my way to the town from our house – we lived on the hillside across the river from Marradi – when I heard the sound of the planes. I immediately knew, something told me, the Americans were coming to bomb the bridges. I turned and ran back to the house to my mother and father; next door lived my aunt and my cousin.

'They're coming to bomb, run away, quick, quick,' I warned.

We ran up the hillside towards a cottage away from the town. My mother couldn't run fast enough and hid under a small shed which was built on stilts. My aunt and cousin hid in a tree.

I watched the planes fly up the valley; they had big white stars on the wings, the sky seemed full of planes. Some German guns, which guarded the bridges, opened fire, but they were few in number.

The bombs started to fall and I heard the scream as they fell. I threw myself flat on the ground and the bombs burst. I could feel the air beat over me and debris all over my head. I thought of my sister and I said, 'Oh, I'm coming to join you.'

When the bombers had finished, there wasn't much left of Marradi, the buildings in the square were flattened and there were fires everywhere. A terrible sound came from the town below, screams and moans of the injured and trapped; men's voices and animals in pain. Those sounds have stayed with me to this day. Many of the people were killed and injured, my aunt and my cousin were among the dead.

There is an old Italian proverb: *Fidari e bene, non fidari e meglio* (To trust is good, not to trust is better); perhaps this helps explain why the forces of extremism, both communist and neo-fascist, were to retain an influence and respectability on the Italian post-war political scene.

Kesselring decreed [that] there should be no sustained defence of precious Florence. Even so, all the bridges across the Arno at Florence were blown with the exception of the Ponte Vecchio, which was blocked by craters and demolished buildings and not strong enough for heavy traffic anyway.

These instructions were 'interpreted' by the soldiers on the ground with typical Teutonic thoroughness. Daniel Lang, a correspondent with *New Yorker* magazine, later described the scene:

The German treatment of Florence amounts to an atrocity story. Most of the city is still standing, but thanks to the enemy's well-placed demolitions, many of the most beloved parts are gone. According to Lt Frederick Hartt, a former Yale art instructor, now serving as the A.M.G.'s Fine Arts and Monuments Officer for this region, about a third of medieval Florence has been destroyed or damaged beyond repair. Much of the section that was always considered the most characteristic of old Florence – the walk along the

Arno, where the thirteenth- and fourteenth-century houses, with their bell towers and enclosed balconies, lined the river's banks – is now rubble . . . With these buildings disappeared their contents, irreplaceable furnishings, invaluable libraries and collections, among them the books and photographs assembled by the late Raimond van Marle, the noted Dutch art historian.

All this destruction can be ascribed to what appears to have been one of the rare attempts of the Germans to preserve *Kultur* outside their own country. As the Allies moved towards the city, the Nazis, using understandable military tactics, decided to destroy the bridges across the Arno to delay our advance. Although they had no hesitation about blowing up the Ponte Santa Trinita, one of the finest of all Renaissance bridges (it resisted three charges of explosives before it fell), they felt the shop-encrusted Ponte Vecchio, which is somewhat reminiscent of Nuremburg architecture, ought to be spared. They were not, however, prepared to cede any military advantages to the Allies. They therefore set demolition charges in the houses at both ends of the bridge, to block it with huge mounds of rubble. To keep the partisans from learning of their plans and possibly deactivating the mines, the Germans gave the occupants of the houses no warning. After the explosions, an uncounted number of corpses lay buried under the ruins, and part of the Via de'Bardi, the Via de'Guicciardini, the Borgo San Jacopo, the Via Por Santa Maria, and several other streets – the heart of Giotto's Florence – were wrecked. Among the more heavily damaged buildings were the Churches of

Santo Stefano and Santa Trinita and the Palazzo di Parte Guelfa, all particularly fine structures. Several of the Uffizi Gallery's sixteenth-century frescoed ceilings fell and the north end of the Pitti Palace is scarred and windowless. Now that the Nazis have begun shelling the city, there will be further destruction.

ERIC MORRIS

SICILIAN INVASION

The mafia isn't just a criminal organization. It is just people with guns. It's a system of power, and it became the formal, legal political system in Sicily at the end of the war. The Americans brought it. It all goes back to 1943 . . .

Around midnight in Sicily they started coming ashore. It was the night between the ninth and the tenth of July, summer on the southern coast between Licata and Gela. It was 1943, a year before the Normandy invasion. The allied armies were making their first European landing. Nine days later Rome was bombed for the first time and five days after that the fascist government fell. Two months after the Sicily landings the new Italian government signed an armistice with the allies and a month later declared war on Germany. As partisans fought the retreating nazis and the fascist rump regime in the north, behind allied lines the political parties of the coming republic took form. In Sicily a rather particular state of affairs prevailed.

Disembarking on the southern coast between Licata and Gela, the US seventh army went through central and western Sicily with curious ease. It took the American troops seven days to secure the mountainous German-occupied island, a little under half the size of Tasmania with ten times the population. Casualties were negligible. General Patton exulted that it was *the fastest blitzkrieg in history*. The unparalleled speed and painlessness of the American operation didn't pass without comment, especially when people compared it with the five-week slog up the east coast of Sicily by the British and Canadian forces under Montgomery, who suffered thousands of losses.

Leoluca Orlando reminded me now of the old story about the allied invasion. The vanguard of the invading Americans, he said, carried flags and foulards of yellow silk, embroidered with the letter *L*. One had been dropped by a low-flying US reconnaissance plane on the hill town of Villalba, at the doorstep of the local priest, brother of don Calogero Vizzini. Don Carlò was about to be made an honorary colonel in the US Army. He was already *capo di tutti i capi*, boss of bosses of the Sicilian mafia and had thirty-nine murders, six attempted murders, thirty-six robberies, thirty-seven thefts, sixty-three extortions on his personal charge sheet. He was heavily into the black market business when the kerchief fell from the sky. As the Americans moved towards Palermo, two thirds of the defending Italian troops deserted. The L had stood for Lucky Luciano, born Salvatore Lucania in 1897 in Licardi Freddi, a treeless, stony sulphur-mining town in Sicily. Lucania was brought to America when he was not quite ten. He was educated in the streets of New York.

His father, he explained, was a laborer in Sicily, and he really believed all those fairy tales about the streets paved with gold in America. He never did admit it was bullshit. 'Christ, we were starving. I was hustlin' in the streets when I was twelve, stealing and runnin' penny-ante crap games . . . You're a kid in the slums, and you see your old man bustin' his hump for peanuts. At the same time you see the local sharpies – the bookies and the tor-pedoes – all makin' dough and drivin' limousines . . . So what's the kid to do? He gotta decide whether he's going to be a crumb, or make dough. Me, I made up my mind pretty young. I'd rather shoot myself than be a crumb.' (from *La Storia*)

At the beginning of 1943, Luciano had been serving a thirty-to-fifty-year sentence in a US penitentiary and was considered the *capo di tutti i capi* of the American Cosa Nostra.

Five months before the allied invasion of Sicily he'd appealed for a reduction of his sentence in return *for services rendered to the nation*. He was said to have been aboard the plane that dropped the foulard. He was certainly released and deported to Italy in 1946. An elderly lawyer once recounted to me his horror and indignation when many years earlier he'd found himself at the next table from Luciano in one of the smartest restaurants in Naples, where Luciano set up residence after the war and where he eventually died in 1962. Luciano was living off contraband drugs and cigarettes, and a Naples police report of 1954 described how his attitude of insolent self-assurance and lack of visible income were a cause for scandal among decent people.

Gore Vidal remarked once that Sicily had been liberated by Lucky Luciano, Vito Genovese *and the American Army*. It was certainly a matter of record that Genovese, Luciano's man in New York and a major drug trafficker of the day, also ended up in Italy at this time, as official interpreter and advisor to the US military governor in Naples.

The British military governor wrote later that 'many of my officers fell into the trap . . . of following the advice of their interpreters.' Who were, he added, mafiosi. A US Army captain, in a worried report of October 1943 on the black market in food supplies, found that the mafia was not merely a criminal organization but also a 'social system, a way of life, a profession.'

The allied landing of 1943, said Sciascia, took place in almost identical conditions to the landing of the Arabs on 16 June 827, with the Germans' Goering division in the place of the Byzantine garrison . . . The island as ever without defences, crushed by a greedy and corrupt administration, terrified of the present and uncertain of the future.

From *Midnight in Sicily*, PETER ROBB

NAPLES

These brigands were the opposition to the vile governments which in Italy took the place of the medieval Republics. Even in our own day, everyone certainly dreads an encounter with brigands; but when they are caught and punished, everyone is sorry for them. The fact is that this people, so shrewd, so cynical, which laughs at everything published under the official censorship of its masters, finds its favourite reading in the little poems which narrate the ardour of the lives of the most renowned brigands. The heroic element that it finds in these stories thrills the artistic vein that still survives in the masses . . . in their heart of hearts, the people were for them, and the village girls preferred to all the rest the boy who once in his life had been obliged *andare alla macchia*, to flee to the woods.

STENDHAL

Naples had no equivalent in Christendom. Her population – 280,000 in 1595 – was twice that of Venice, three times that of Rome, four times that of Florence, and nine times that of Marseilles. The whole of southern Italy flocked to the city, both the rich, often very rich, and the hopelessly wretched poor. The size of the population was one reason why so many luxury goods were produced there. Neapolitan goods in the sixteenth century were what would be called fancy goods today: lace, braids, frills, trimmings, silks, light fabrics (taffetas), silken knots and cockades of all colours, and fine linens. These goods travelled as far as Cologne in large quantities. The Venetians claimed that four-fifths of the workers of Naples lived off the silk industry, and we know that the *Arte di Santa Lucia* enjoyed a great reputation over a wide area. Pieces of so-called Santa Lucia silk were even resold at Florence. In 1642 the proposal of sumptuary laws in Spain, which would have threatened Neapolitan exports of silk and silken goods, endangered the annual fiscal income of 335,220 ducats. But there were many other industries either already established in the city or which the vast labour force could have attracted there.

Peasants from throughout the provinces of the vast, mountainous, and pastoral kingdom flocked into the city. They were
attracted by the *arti* of wool and silk; by the city's public works
begun in the time of Pietro di Toledo and carried on long after
him (some buildings were still unfinished in 1594); by domestic employment in the household of nobles, for it was becoming
the fashion for aristocrats to live in the city and display their
wealth; if all else failed, they could always rely upon the countless religious establishments with their throngs of servants and
hangers-on. By seeking employment in the city, which was to be
had 'in all seasons', the peasants automatically released themselves from heavy feudal obligations to an overlord who might
have inherited or bought, as Genoese merchants frequently did,
his title and estates, which were always on the market. As the
proverb says, 'the city air brings freedom' – but not necessarily
happiness or a full stomach. So the city continued to grow.

FERNAND BRAUDEL

Naples in 1995 still seemed an utterly disoriented city whose
language and gestures remained what they'd been but no longer
referred to reality.

A poison was abroad in Naples now. Resentments surfaced
quickly. The baroque configuration of the Neapolitan mind
was being twisted further into something ugly. Meanwhile you
were expected to admire pedestrian zones and open air cafes.
The theme park necrosis was taking hold. Sinister forces wanted
to embalm the city, create another Venice, a little piece of
Tuscany. People were being pushed to the edges, if not out of
town. You could see them in the shadows, at the edge of your

field of vision. Was it the beauty that blurred my eyes now, or the life gone from the place I'd known? Naples had never seemed more beautiful. I felt like a ghost stalking the streets. *The tourists are coming back!* Twenty years earlier, Naples had been a dying city that belonged to the people who lived there. It was hardly bearable at best, yet there'd been life in the dreadfulness of life. You seldom heard Neapolitan now. The absurd comedy was gone. Naples broke my heart. And yet, as the city always had, it teased, it led you on to dream of more than it would ever deliver, made you remember why you'd thrown away your life to be there and still, for an instant, if you loved it, think it the most marvellous city in the world. In Naples you remembered being happy and never why. Naples, I consoled myself with thinking, would always be more *interesting* than other places. Naples would never bore. When Braudel saw Naples at its nadir in 1983, he reflected that, 'Naples had always scandalized, scandalized and seduced . . . Italy's lost a lot from not knowing, out of indifference and also fear, how to use the formidable potential of this city, which is really too different, European more than Italian . . .'

Naples was the only place I'd ever felt at home.

PETER ROBB

Norman Lewis arrived in Naples as an Intelligence Officer attached to the American Fifth Army. By 1944 the inhabitants were so destitute that all the tropical fish in the city's aquarium had been devoured, and even respectable women were driven to prostitution. The mafia gradually became so indispensable to the occupying forces that it succeeded in regaining its former power. Despite the cruelty and suffering he encountered, Norman Lewis writes in his diary, 'A year among the Italians has converted me to such an admiration of their humanity and culture that were I given the chance to be born again, Italy would be the country of my choice.'

October 6
The city of Naples smells of charred wood, with ruins everywhere, sometimes completely blocking the streets, bomb craters and abandoned trams. The main problem is water. Two tremendous air-raids on August 4 and September 6 smashed up all the services, and there has been no proper water supply since the first of these. To complete the Allies' work of destruction, German demolition squads have gone round blowing up anything of value to the city that still worked. Such has been the great public thirst of the past few days that we are told that people have experimented with sea-water in their cooking, and families have been seen squatting along the sea-shore round weird contraptions with which they hope to distil sea-water for drinking purposes.

The Section has fallen on its feet. I arrived to find that we had been installed in the Palace of the Princes of Satriano at the end of Naples' impressive seafront, the Riviera di Chiaia, in the Piazza Vittoria. The four-storey building is in the Neapolitan version of Spanish baroque, and we occupy its principal floor at the head of a sweep of marble staircase, with high ceilings decorated with mouldings, glittering chandeliers, enormous wall-mirrors, and opulent gilded furniture in vaguely French-Empire style. There are eight majestic rooms, but no bathroom, and the lavatory is in a cupboard in the kitchen. The view across the square is of clustered palms, much statuary, and the Bay of Naples. The FSO has done very well by us.

There were military units by the dozen all round Naples who wished to employ Italian civilians and all of these had to be vetted by us as security risks. Nothing could have been easier than this operation. The Fascist police state kept close tabs on the activities of all its citizens, and we inherited their extensive archives on the top floor of the Questura – the central police office. Ninety-nine per cent of the information recorded there was numbingly unimportant, and revealed as a whole that most Italians lead political lives of utter neutrality, although prone to sexual adventures. In all, the unending chronicles of empty lives.

October 9
This afternoon, another trip along the sea-front at Santa Lucia provided a similar spectacle of the desperate hunt for food. Rocks were piled up here against the sea wall and innumerable children were at work among them. I learned that they were prising limpets off the rocks, all the winkles and sea-snails.

October 15
Among the civilian contacts of these first few days, my prize acquisition was Vincente Lattarullo, a man steeped in the knowledge of the ways of Naples.

When originally asked what was his business with us, he answered in a dry whisper, 'I am motivated by the passion for justice,' and, saying this, he appeared to vibrate. It turned out that this distinguished, fragile-looking man, who sometimes halted in mid-sentence and swayed a little, as if about to faint, wished to denounce the activities of an American requisitioning officer who was going round offering Italian car-owners a guarantee against their cars being requisitioned on payment of 100,000 lire. We told him that there was absolutely nothing we could do about it.

I took him to the Bar Vittoria next door for a *marsala all'uovo*, but when the barman brought the egg to be broken into his glass I saw the anguish in Lattarullo's face, and stopped him in mid-action. Apologies streamed forth and then Lattarullo begged to be allowed to take the egg home. Moments later the impact of the alcohol on an empty stomach set him swaying again and I realized that the man was starving. Unfortunately there was no food of any kind anywhere within range, except the prized and precious eggs, rationed on a basis of one per day to favoured customers. However, Lattarullo was prevailed upon to accept my egg as well, which he beat up in a cup, and swallowed very slowly there and then.

He proved to be one of the four thousand lawyers of Naples, ninety per cent of whom – surplus to the needs of the courts – had never practised, and who for the most part lived in extreme penury. There are estimated to be at least as many medical doctors in a similar situation; these famished professionals being the end-product of the determination of every middle-class Neapolitan family to have a uselessly qualified son. The parents are prepared to go hungry so long as the son is entitled to be addressed with respect as *avvocato*, or *dottore*.

Lattarullo had succeeded in staying alive on a legacy originally worth about a pound a week, now reduced by devaluation to about five shillings, and in order to do this had worked out a scientific system of self-restraints. He stayed most of the day in bed, and when he got up walked short distances along a planned itinerary, stopping to rest every few hundred yards in a church. He ate an evening meal only, normally composed of a little bread dipped in olive oil, into which was rubbed a tomato. Sometimes he visited another professional man in similar circumstances and they exchanged gossip, sipped a cup of coffee made from roasted acorns, and starved socially for an hour or so. He gave the impression that he knew everything that was going on in Naples. I walked back to his flat with him, and found him living in two rooms containing three chairs, a bed, and a rickety table on which stood an embittered aspidistra plant. The lighting and the water had been cut off years ago, he said.

It appeared that Lattarullo had a secondary profession producing occasional windfalls of revenue. This had to be suspended in the present emergency. He admitted with a touch of pride to acting as a *Zio di Roma* – an 'uncle from Rome' – at funerals. Neapolitan funerals are obsessed with face. A man who may have been a near-pauper all his life is certain to be put away in a magnificent coffin, but apart from that no other little touch likely to honour the dead and increase the bereaved family's prestige is overlooked.

The uncle from Rome is a popular character in this little farce. Why should people insist on Rome? Why not Bari or Taranto? But no, Rome it has to be. The uncle lets it be known that he has just arrived on the Rome express, or he shows up at the slum tenement or lowly *basso* in an Alfa-romeo with a Roman number-plate and an SPQR badge, out of which he steps in his well-cut morning suit, on the jacket lapel of which he sports the ribbon of a Commendatore of the Crown of Italy, to temper with his restrained and dignified condolences the theatrical display of Neapolitan grief.

Lattarullo said that he had frequently played this part. His qualifications were his patrician appearance, and a studied Roman accent and manner. Where the Neapolitans tend to familiarity and ingratiation, Lattarullo shows a proper Roman aloofness and taciturnity. When Lattarullo meets a man he says *buon giorno* and leaves it at that, and he goes off with a curt goodbye. This, say the Neapolitans, who are fulsome and cloying in their greetings, is how a real Roman gentleman speaks.

October 20
A narrow escape today while motor-cycling along the Via Partenope. I was riding towards the Castel Nuovo, through an area badly damaged by bombing, with the sea on the right and semi-derelict buildings on the left, when I noticed a sudden change ahead from blue sky, sunshine and shadow, to a great opaque whiteness, shutting off the view of the port. The effect was one of a whole district blotted out by a pall of the white smoke sometimes spread from the chimneys of a factory producing lime. On turning a bend, I came upon an apocalyptic scene. A number of buildings including a bank had been pulverized by a terrific explosion that had clearly just taken place. Bodies were scattered all over the street, but here and there

among them stood the living, as motionless as statues and all coated in thick white dust. What engraved this scene on the mind and the imagination was that nothing moved, and that the silence was total. Dust drifted down from the sky like a most delicate snowfall. A woman stood like Lot's wife turned to salt beside a cart drawn by two mules. One mule lay apparently dead, the other stood quietly at its side, without so much as twitching an ear. Nearby two men lay in the positions of bodies overcome by ash at Pompeii, and a third, who had probably been in their company, stood swaying very slightly, his eyes shut. I spoke to him, but he did not reply. There was no blood to be seen anywhere.

November 5

In 1835 Alexander Dumas, who spent some weeks in Naples, wrote of its upper classes that only four families enjoyed great fortunes, that twenty were comfortably off, and the rest had to struggle to make ends meet. What mattered was to have a well-painted carriage harnessed up to a couple of old horses, a coachman in threadbare livery, and a private box at the San Carlo – where the social life of the town was largely conducted. People lived in their carriages or in the theatre, but their houses were barred to visitors, and hermetically sealed, as Dumas puts it, against foreigners like himself.

He discovered that all but a tiny handful of the ancient families of Naples lived in straitened circumstances, and this is roughly the situation a century later. They talked in a matter-of-fact and quite convincing way of the golden days of their families under Imperial Rome, but they had not enough to eat.

The Neapolitan upper-crust of those times consumed only one meal every twenty-four hours; at two in the afternoon in winter, and at midnight in summer. Their food was almost as poor in quality and as monotonous as that served to prisoners in gaol: invariably with a little fish, and washed down with Asprino d'Aversa, tasting – according to Dumas – more like rough cider than wine. By way of an occasional extravagance, one of these pauper-noblemen might force himself to go without bread or macaroni for a day, and spend what he had saved on an ice-cream to be eaten splendidly, in public, at the fashionable Café Donzelli.

November 10

The sexual attitudes of Neapolitans never fail to produce new surprises. Today Prince A., now well known to us all and an enthusiastic informant from our first days at the Riviera di Chiaia, visited us with his sister, whom we met for the first time. The Prince is the absentee landlord of a vast estate somewhere in the South, and owns a nearby palace stacked with family portraits and Chinese antiques. He is the head of what is regarded as the second or third noble family of Southern Italy. The Prince is about thirty years of age, and his sister could be twenty-four. Both are remarkably alike in appearance: thin, with extremely pale skin and cold, patrician expressions bordering on severity. The purpose of the visit was to enquire if we could arrange for the sister to enter an army brothel. We explained that there was no such institution in the British Army. 'A pity,' the Prince said. Both of them speak excellent English, learned from an English governess. 'Ah, well, Luisa, I suppose if it can't be, it can't be.' They thanked us with polite calm, and departed.

Last week a section member was invited by a female contact to visit the Naples cemetery with her on the coming Sunday afternoon. Informants have to be cultivated in small ways whenever possible, and he was quite prepared to indulge a whim of this kind, in the belief that he would he escorting his friend on a visit to a family tomb, expecting to buy a bunch of chrysanthemums from the stall at the gate. However, hardly were they inside when the lady dragged him behind a tomb-stone, and then – despite the cold – lay down and pulled up her skirts. He noticed that the cemetery contained a number of other couples in vigorous activity in broad daylight. 'There were more people above ground than under it,' he said. It turned out that the cemetery is the lovers' lane of Naples, and the custom is such that one becomes invisible as soon as one passes through the gates. If a visitor runs into anyone he knows neither a sign nor a glance can be exchanged, nor does one recognize any friend encountered on the 133 bus which goes to the cemetery. I have learned that to suggest to a lady a Sunday-afternoon ride on a 133 bus is tantamount to solicitation for immoral purposes.

November 25

Food, for the Neapolitans, comes even before love, and its pur-suit is equally insatiable and ingenious. They are almost as adaptable, too, as the Chinese in the matter of the food-stuffs they are prepared to consume. A contact from Nola mentioned that the villages in his area had lost all their breeding storks because last year the villagers eked out shortages by eating their nestlings. This is regarded as a calamity by those who did not benefit directly, as there is a widespread and superstitious aversion in Italy, as elsewhere, to molesting storks in any way.

Another example of culinary enterprise was provided by the consumption of all the tropical fish in Naples' celebrated aquarium in the days preceding the liberation, no fish being spared, however strange and specialized its appearance and habits. All Neapolitans believe that at the banquet offered to welcome General Mark Clark – who had expressed a preference for fish – the principal course was a baby manatee – the most prized item of the aquarium's collection – which was boiled and served with a garlic sauce. These two instances demonstrate a genius for improvisation. But some of the traditional local cooking is weird enough in its own right. On Vesuvius they make a soft cheese to which lamb's intestine is added. Shrove Tuesday's speciality is *sanguinaccio* – pig's blood cooked with chocolate and herbs.

My experience of Neapolitan gastronomy was expanded by an invitation to a dinner, the main feature of which was a spaghetti-eating competition. Such contests have been a normal feature of social life, latterly revived and raised almost to the level of a cult as a result of the reappearance on the black market of the necessary raw materials.

March 15
There has been an issue to the troops of leaflets printed in Italian to be handed to any tout approaching a soldier to offer the services of a prostitute. It begins: 'I am not interested in

your syphilitic sister.' Whoever dreamed this one up clearly had no idea of some of the implications or the possible consequences. Remarks about sisters are strictly taboo to Southern Italians, and the final insult *tu sora* (thy sister) is calculated instantly to produce a duel or vendetta. Many soldiers have already handed over these dangerous notices to people who accosted them for reasons other than prostitution, and there are bound to be casualties.

March 19
Today Vesuvius erupted. It was the most majestic and terrible sight I have ever seen, or expect to see. The smoke from the crater slowly built up into a great bulging shape having all the appearance of solidity. It swelled and expanded so slowly that there was no sign of movement in the cloud which, by evening, must have risen thirty or forty thousand feet into the sky, and measured many miles across.

The shape of the eruption that obliterated Pompeii reminded Pliny of a pine tree, and he probably stood here at Posillipo across the bay, where I was standing now and where Nelson and Emma Hamilton stood to view the eruption of their day, and the shape was indeed like that of a many-branching tree. What took one by surprise about Pliny's pine was that it was absolutely motionless, not quite painted – because it was three-dimensional – but moulded on the sky; an utterly still, and utterly menacing shape. This pine, too, trailed uncharacteristically a little tropical liana of heavy ash, which fell earthwards here and there from its branches in imperceptible motion.

At night the lava streams began to trickle down the mountain's slopes. By day the spectacle was calm but now the eruption showed a terrible vivacity. Fiery symbols were scrawled across the water of the bay, and periodically the crater discharged mines of serpents into a sky which was the deepest of blood reds and pulsating everywhere with lighning reflections.

From *Naples '44*, NORMAN LEWIS

ON MACHIAVELLI'S THE PRINCE

. . . preoccupied with politics, every man to his own passion, from the porter in the market-place to the barber in his shop or the artisans in the taverns; for *raggione di stato, raison d'état,* an Italian rediscovery, was the result not of isolated reflection but of collective experience. Similarly, the frequent cruelty in political affairs, the betrayals and renewed flames of personal vendettas are so many symptoms of an age when the old governmental structures were breaking up and a series of new ones appearing in rapid succession, according to circumstances beyond man's control. These were days when justice was frequently an absent figure and governments were too new and too insecure to dispense with force and emergency measures. Terror was a means of government. *The Prince* taught the art of day-to-day survival.

FERNAND BRAUDEL

CRUELTY AND COMPASSION; AND WHETHER IT IS BETTER TO BE LOVED THAN FEARED, OR THE REVERSE

Taking others of the qualities I enumerated above, I say that a prince should want to have a reputation for compassion rather than for cruelty: nonetheless, he should be careful that he does not make bad use of compassion. Cesare Borgia was accounted cruel; nevertheless, this cruelty of his reformed the Romagna, brought it unity, and restored order and obedience. On reflection, it will be seen that there was more compassion in Cesare than in the Florentine people, who, to escape being called cruel, allowed Pistoia to be devastated. So a prince should not worry if he incurs reproach for his cruelty so long as he keeps his subjects united and loyal. By making an example or two he will prove more compassionate than those who, being too compassionate, allow disorders which lead to murder and rapine. These nearly always harm the whole community, whereas executions ordered by a prince only affect individuals. A new prince, of all rulers, finds it impossible to avoid a reputation for cruelty, because of the abundant dangers inherent in a newly won state.

Nonetheless, a prince should be slow to take action, and should watch that he does not come to be afraid of his own shadow; his behaviour should be tempered by humanity and prudence so that overconfidence does not make him rash or excessive distrust make him unbearable.

From this arises the following question: whether it is better to be loved than feared, or the reverse. The answer is that one would like to be both the one and the other; but because it is difficult to combine them, it is far better to be feared than loved if you cannot be both. One can make this generalization about men: they are ungrateful, fickle, liars, and deceivers, they shun danger and are greedy for profit; while you treat them well, they are yours. They would shed their blood for you, risk their property, their lives, their children, so long, as I said above, as danger is remote; but when you are in danger they turn against you. Any prince who has come to depend entirely on promises and has taken no other precautions ensures his own ruin; friendship which is bought with money and not with greatness and nobility of mind is paid for, but it does not last and it yields nothing. Men worry less about doing an injury to one who makes himself loved than to one who makes himself feared. The bond of love is one which men, wretched creatures that they are, break when it is to their advantage to do so; but fear is strengthened by a dread of punishment which is always effective.

The prince should nonetheless make himself feared in such a way that, if he is not loved, at least he escapes being hated. For fear is quite compatible with an absence of hatred; and the prince can always avoid hatred if he abstains from the property of his subjects and citizens and from their women. If, even so, it proves necessary to execute someone, this should be done only when there is proper justification and manifest reason for it. But above all a prince should abstain from the property of others; because men sooner forget the death of their father than the loss of their patrimony.

From *The Prince*, NICCOLO MACHIAVELLI

A IR

In volo, la terra, il cielo ed io tra loro.
(In flight, the earth, the sky and I between them)

GENNARO NUNZIANTE

All the movements of the wind resemble those of the water. Universally all things desire to maintain their natural state.

Write how the clouds are formed and how they dissolve, and what it is that causes vapour to rise from the water of the earth into the air, and the cause of mists and of the air becoming thickened, and why it appears more blue or less blue at one time than at another.

[Smoke] . . . enters into the air in the form of a wave, like that which water . . . its force causes it to burst through other water.

From *The Notebooks of Leonardo da Vinci*

Wagner has lovely moments but awful quarters of an hour.

ROSSINI

I have always carried with me a large bundle of melancholy. I have no reason for it, but so I am made.

PUCCINI

Viareggio
22 October 1924

Dear Adamino,

What shall I tell you? I am going through a most terrible time. That trouble in my throat torments me more morally than physically. I am going to Brussels to consult a famous specialist. I am leaving soon . . . Will they operate on me? shall I be cured? Or condemned to death? I cannot go on like this any longer. And then there is *Turandot* . . .

Puccini at a meeting in Milan with Toscanini:

My opera will be given incomplete, and then someone will come on the stage and say to the public, 'At this point the composer died!'

From *Puccini: a critical biography*, MOSCO CARNER

Walter Starkie [described] Gabriele d'Annunzio as 'a dwarf of a man, goggle-eyed and thick-lipped – truly sinister in his grotesqueness, like a tragic gargoyle. Is this the man that [Duse] loved?' But his voice played upon the emotions of the crowd as a supreme violinist does upon a Stradivarius.

Little by little, however, I began to sink under the fascination of the voice, which penetrated into my consciousness, syllable by syllable, like water from a clear fountain. It was a slow precise voice, accompanying the words right to the last vowel as if he wished to savour to the utmost their echoing music. The tones rose and fell in an unending stream, like the song of a minstrel, and they spread over the vast audience like olive oil on the surface of the sea.

  From *Gabriele d'Annunzio, Defiant Archangel,* JOHN WOODHOUSE

As I was returning home late one night on the gloomy canal, the moon appeared suddenly and illuminated the marvellous palaces and the tall figure of my gondolier towering above the stern of the gondola, slowly moving his huge sweep. Suddenly he uttered a deep wail, not unlike the cry of an animal; the cry gradually gained in strength, and formed itself, after a long-drawn 'Oh!' into the simple musical exclamation 'Venezia!' This was followed by other sounds of which I have no distinct rec-ollection, as I was so much moved at the time. Such were the impressions that to me appeared the most characteristic of Venice during my stay there, and they remained with me until the completion of the second act of *Tristan,* and possibly even suggested to me the long-drawn wail of the shepherd's horn at the beginning of the third act.

WAGNER

Music lives only in Italy.

STENDHAL

During the night I had a strange experience. We were dead tired and had thrown ourselves on our beds in an inn which was anything but elegant. At midnight I woke up and saw over my head a star so beautiful that I thought I had never seen one like it. Its enchanting light seemed a prophecy of good things to come and my spirit felt utterly refreshed, but soon it disappeared, leaving me alone in the dark. It was not till day-break that I discovered what had caused this miracle. There was a crack in the roof and I had woken up just at the very moment when one of the most beautiful stars in the firmament was crossing my private meridian. The travellers, of course, unhesitatingly interpreted this natural phenomenon as an omen in their favour.

From *Italian Journey*, GOETHE

THE CAPPUCCINI

I was playing near the church of the Capuchins, with some other children who were all younger than myself. There was fastened on the church door a little cross of metal; it was fastened about the middle of the door, and I could just reach it with my hand. Always when our mothers had passed by with us they had lifted us up that we might kiss the holy sign. One day, when we children were playing, one of the youngest of them inquired, why the child Jesus did not come down and play with us? I assumed an air of wisdom, and replied that he was really bound upon the cross. We went to the church door, and although we found no one, we wished, as our mothers had taught us, to kiss him, but we could not reach up to it; one therefore lifted up the other, but just as the lips were pointed for the kiss, that one who lifted the other lost his strength, and the kissing one fell down just when his lips were about to touch the invisible child Jesus. At that moment my mother came by, and when she saw our child's play, she folded her hands, and said, 'You are actually some of God's angels, and thou art mine own angel,' added she, and kissed me.

The Capuchin monk, Fra Martino, was my mother's confessor. He made very much of me, and gave me a picture of the Virgin, weeping great tears, which fell, like rain-drops, down into the burning flames of hell, where the damned caught this draught of refreshment. He took me over with him into the convent, where the open colonnade, which enclosed in a square the little potato-garden, with the two cypress and orange-trees, made a very deep impression upon me. Side by side, in the open passages, hung old portraits of deceased monks, and on the doors of each cell were pasted pictures from the history of the martyrs, which I contemplated with the same holy emotions as afterwards the masterpieces of Raphael and Andrea del Sarto.

'Thou art really a bright youth,' said he; 'thou shalt now see the dead.' Upon this, he opened a little door of a gallery which lay a few steps below the colonnade. We descended, and now I saw round about me skulls upon skulls, so placed one upon another, that they formed walls, and therewith several chapels. In these were regular niches, in which were seated perfect skeletons of the most distinguished of the monks, enveloped in their brown cowls, their cords round their waists, and with a breviary or withered bunch of flowers in their hands. Altars, chandeliers, bas-reliefs, of human joints, horrible and tasteless as the whole idea. I clung fast to the monk, who whispered a prayer, and then said to me, 'Here also I shall some time sleep; wilt thou thus visit me?'

255

I answered not a word, but looked horrified at him, and then round about me upon the strange grizzly assembly. It was foolish to take me, a child, into this place. I was singularly impressed with the whole thing, and did not feel myself easy again until I came into his little cell, where the beautiful yellow oranges almost hung at the window, and I saw the brightly coloured picture of the Madonna, who was borne upwards by angels into the clear sunshine, while a thousand flowers filled the grave in which she had rested . . .

On the festival of All-Saints I was down in the chapel of the dead, where Fra Martino took me when I first visited the convent. All the monks sang masses for the dead, and I, with two other boys of my own age, swung the incense-breathing censer before the great altar of skulls. They had placed lights in the chandeliers made of bones, new garlands were placed round the brows of the skeleton monks, and fresh bouquets in their hands. Many people, as usual, thronged in; they all knelt and the singers intoned the solemn *Miserere*. I gazed for a long time on the pale yellow skulls, and the fumes of the incense which wavered in strange shapes between me and them, and everything began to swim round before my eyes; it was as if I saw everything through a large rainbow; as if a thousand prayer-bells rung in my ear; it seemed as if I was borne along a stream; it was unspeakably delicious. More, I know not; consciousness left me – I was in a swoon.

From *Walks in Rome*, REV. AUGUSTUS J.C. HARE

The summer epidemics. But the hot weather also caused fresh outbreaks of the endemic diseases that only temporarily subsided in winter. Baron de Tott notes that the plague 'begins its ravages in the spring and usually lasts until the beginning of winter.' As usual, the towns were the most threatened. Every summer Rome was a graveyard of fever. So the cardinals took refuge in their country houses, their *vigne*, which were not merely an ostentatious luxury.

FERNAND BRAUDEL

Of the soul
Movement of earth against earth pressing down upon it causes a slight movement of the parts struck.

Water struck by water creates circles at a great distance round the spot where it is struck; the voice in the air goes further, in fire further still; mind ranges over the universe but being finite it does not extend into infinity.

He who does not value life does not deserve it. It is not necessary for any of the elements which invest one another to be of equal size in all its extent as between that part that invests and that which is invested.

Moreover, as regards the air which clothes the sphere of the water together with the mountains and valleys which rise about this sphere, there is not left any vacuum between the land and the air.

The body of the air is filled with an infinite number of radiant pyramids formed by the objects situated in it . . .

The elements are changed one into another, and when the air is changed into water by the contact it has with its cold region this then attracts to itself with fury all the surrounding air which

257

moves furiously to fill up the place vacated by the air that has escaped; and so one mass moves in succession behind another, until they have in part equalised the space from which the air has been divided, and this is the wind.

Of winds

The north wind comes to us from high and frozen places and therefore it cannot give off moisture, and consequently it is pure and clean, because it is cold and dry, and for this reason it is very light in itself but its speed makes it powerful wherever it strikes.

The south wind has not the same purity, and since it is warm and dry it dissolves the thicknesses of the watery vapours which the Mediterranean Sea exhales, and these then follow in the wake of this wind and become dissolved in it; and so for this reason this wind as it strikes Europe comes to be warm and damp and heavy in its nature, and although its movement is sluggish its stroke is no less powerful than that of the north wind.

Of flame and wind

Where flame cannot live no animal that draws breath can live. Excess of wind puts out flame, moderate wind nourishes it.

The bottom part of the flame is the first beginning of this flame through which passes all its nutriment of fat; and this is of so much less heat than the rest of the flame as it is of less brightness; and it is blue in colour and is the part in which its nutriment is purged and disposed of.

That wind will be of briefer movement which is of more impetuous beginning.

The images of every visible object are all infused in all the air over against them, and are all separated in every part of the same air.

The images of objects which confusedly as they mingle fill with themselves the air over against them are all in all this air and all in every part of it.

The fifth essence is infused through the air as is the element of fire, although each of these may have its reason in itself or through itself.

The colours of the middle of the rainbow mingle with each other.

Of the wind

Many are the times when the course of one wind is diverted into that of another, and this arises from the percussion which they make at the meeting of their courses when as they are not able to penetrate into the other necessity constrains them to leap back in opposite directions.

If however the said winds are not of equal power one with another their reflex movements will not follow the movement of their striker, but the angle of percussion of the more powerful will be as much greater than that of the less powerful as is the excess of the greater power over the lesser.

Winds which blow in the same direction may be simple or mixed with other winds.

Whether the curves of the end parts of the wing are necessary or not
The air which is underneath the curves of the end parts of the wing as they descend is more compressed than any other portion of the air that is found underneath the bird, and this is brought about by the beating of the wings.

The air itself is capable of being compressed and rarefied to an infinite degree.

From *The Notebooks of Leonardo da Vinci*

KEATS AMONG THE ANGELS

I am a person who is very often alone. Of the sixteen hours of daily wakefulness, at least ten are spent in solitude. And being unable, after all, to read the whole time, I amuse myself by constructing literary theories . . . such as my theory of the 'angels'.

From time to time there appear on this earth beings whose existence radiates a superhuman light. But to belong to this very restricted elite, genius alone is not sufficient. Neither Shakespeare nor Dante nor Michelangelo nor Baudelaire are among the angels. Maybe they are gods but they are not angels.

To be included among their number it is necessary to die very young or to cease all activity at an early age. One condition, it goes without saying, is that their work is of supreme value, while another is that their presence is short and brilliant, so that they leave us grey mortals with the sensation that they are superhuman visitors who watched us for an instant and then returned to the heavens, bequeathing us gifts of divine quality and also a bitter regret at the fleetingness of the apparition.

Among the 'angels' I place Raphael and Masaccio, Mozart and Hölderlin, Rimbaud and Maurice de Guérin, Shelley, Marlowe and Keats (as you can see, the 'angels' ethics do not concern me). Rupert Brooke and Novalis have just missed promotion to this group, along with Giorgione and Van Gogh. Péguy had the right qualifications to become an angel except that he died too late; Sergio Corazzini died at the right time but did not have sufficient talent. 'Women angels' abound, but they are a very different species.

The first named are indisputably the true 'angels.' In this list, shining with joy and for us tears, the supreme place goes to John Keats. Of all of them, he alone is absolutely pure. I know it is not their fault, but a few spots of mud stain the wings of Marlowe and Shelley. Rimbaud is undoubtedly an angel but, like Marlowe, one is not sure if he comes from above or from below. Raphael's lechery, Hölderlin's madness, Masaccio's bad temper and Mozart's wife are faint blemishes on the whiteness of their clothing. But angel of the first degree, archangel, seraphim, cherubim, angel in full relief, angel of one hundred carats, angel with top-quality wings guaranteed against moths – the only one is John Keats.

From *The Siren and Selected Writings*, GIUSEPPE DI LAMPEDUSA

A false idea of Florence grew up in the nineteenth century, thanks in great part to the Brownings and their readers – a tooled-leather idea of Florence as a dear bit of the old world. Old

maids of both sexes – retired librarians, governesses, ladies
with reduced incomes, gentlemen painters, gentlemen sculptors,
gentlemen poets, anaemic amateurs and dabblers of every kind –
'fell in love' with Florence and settled down to make it home.
Queen Victoria did water colours in the hills at Vincigliata;
Florence Nightingale's parents named her after the city, where she
was born in 1820 – a sugary statue of her stands holding a lamp
in the first cloister of Santa Croce. Early in the present century,
a retired colonel, G.F. Young of the Indian Service, who, it is said,
was unable to read Italian, appointed himself defender of the
Medicis and turned out a spluttering 'classic' that went through
many editions, arguing that the Medicis had been misrepre-
sented by democratic historians. (There is a story in Turgenev of
a retired major who used to practice doctoring on the peasants.
'Has he studied medicine?' someone asks. 'No, he hasn't studied,'
is the answer. 'He does it more from philanthropy.' This was
evidently the case with Colonel Young.) Colonel Young was
typical of the Anglo-American visitors who, as it were, expropri-
ated Florence, occupying villas in Fiesole or Bellosguardo,
studying Tuscan wild flowers, collecting ghost stories, collecting
triptychs and diptychs, burying their dogs in the churchyard of
the Protestant Episcopal church, knowing (for the most part) no
Florentines but their servants. The Brownings, in Casa Guidi,
opposite the Pitti Palace, revelled in Florentine history and hated
the Austrian usurper, who lived across the street, but they did not
mingle socially with the natives; they kept themselves to
themselves. George Eliot spent fifteen days in a Swiss *pensione* on
Via Tornabuoni, conscientiously working up the background
for *Romola*, a sentimental pastiche of Florentine history that was

a great success in its period and is the least read of her novels today. It smelled of libraries, Henry James complained, and the foreign colony's notion of Florence, like *Romola*, was bookish, synthetic, gushing, insular, genteel, and, above all, proprietary. This sickly love ('our Florence,' 'my Florence') on the part of the foreign residents implied, like all such loves, a tyrannous resistance to change. The rest of the world might alter, but, in the jealous eyes of its foreign owners, Florence was supposed to stay exactly as it was when they found it – a dear bit of the Old World.

Florence can never have been that, at any time in its existence. It is not a shrine of the past, and it rebuffs all attempts to make it into one, just as it rebuffs tourists. Tourism, in a certain sense, is an accidental by-product of the city – at once profitable and a nuisance, adding to the noise and congestion, raising prices for the population. Florence is a working city, a market centre, a railway junction; it manufactures furniture (including antiques), shoes, gloves, handbags, textiles, fine underwear, nightgowns, and table linens, picture frames, luggage, chemicals, optical equipment, machinery, wrought iron, various novelties in straw. Much of this work is done in small shops on the Oltrarno, the Florentine Left Bank, or on the farms of the *ontado*; there is not much big industry but there is a multitude of small crafts and trades. Every Friday is market day on the Piazza della Signoria, and the peasants come with pockets full of samples from the farms in the Valdarno and the Chianti: grain, oil, wine, seeds. The small hotels and cheap restaurants are full of commercial travellers, wine salesmen from Certaldo of Siena, textile representatives from Prato, dealers in marble from the

Carrara mountains, where Michelangelo quarried. Everyone is on the move, buying, selling, delivering, and tourists get in the way of this diversified commerce. The Florentines, on the whole, would be happy to be rid of them. The shopkeepers on the Lungarno and on Ponte Vecchio, the owners of hotels and restaurants, the thieves, and the widows who run *pensiones* might regret their departure, but the tourist is seldom led to suspect this. There is no city in Italy that treats its tourists so summarily, that caters so little to their comfort.

There are no gay bars or smart outdoor cafés; there is very little night life, very little vice. The food in the restaurants is bad, for the most part, monotonous, and rather expensive. Many of the Florentine specialities – tripe, paunch, rabbit, and a mixture of the combs, livers, hearts, and testicles of roosters – do not appeal to the foreign palate. The wine can be good but is not so necessarily. The waiters are slapdash and hurried; like many Florentines, they give the impression of being preoccupied with something else, something more important – a knotty thought, a problem. At one of the 'typical' restaurants, recommended by the big hotels, the waiters, who are family, treat the clients like interlopers, feigning not to notice their presence, bawling orders sarcastically to the kitchen, banging down the dishes, spitting on the floor. 'Take it or leave it' is the attitude of the *pensione*-keeper of the better sort when showing a room; the inferior *pensiones* have a practice of shanghaiing tourists. Runners from these establishments lie in wait on the road, just outside the city limits, for cars with foreign licence plates; they halt them, leap aboard, and order the driver to proceed to a certain address. Strangely enough, the tourists often comply, and report to the police only later, when they have been cheated in the *pensiones*.

These shades of Dante's highwaymen are not the only ones who lie in wait for travellers. One of the best Florentine restaurants was closed by the police a few years ago – for cheating a tourist. Complaints of foreign tourists pour every day into the *questura* and are recorded in the morning newspaper; they have been robbed and victimized everywhere; their cars, parked on the Piazza della Signoria or along the Arno, have been rifled in broad daylight or spirited away. The northern races – Germans and Swedes – appear to be the chief prey, and the commonest complaint is of the theft of a camera. Other foreigners are the victims of accidents; one old American lady, the mother-in-law of an author, walking on Via Guicciardini, had the distinction of being hit by two bicycles, from the front and rear simultaneously (she was thrown into the air and suffered a broken arm); some British tourists were injured a few years ago by a piece falling off Palazzo Bartolini Salimbeni (1517–20) in Piazza Santa Trinita. Finally, the sidewalk in front of that crumbling building was closed off and a red lantern posted: beware of falling masonry.* Recently, during the summer, a piece weighing 132 pounds fell off the cornice of the National Library; a bus-conductor, though, rather than a tourist or foreign student, just missed getting killed and, instead, had his picture in the paper.

. . . On the street, the Florentines do not like to give directions; if you are lost, you had better ask a policeman. Unlike the Venetians, the Florentines will never volunteer to show a sight

---

*The palace has since been restored.

to a passing stranger. They do not care to exhibit their city; the monuments are there – let the foreigners find them. Nor is this a sign of indifference, but of a peculiar pride and dignity. Florentine sacristans can never be found to turn on the lights to illuminate a fresco or an altar painting; they do not seem to be interested in the tip. Around the Masolino-Masaccio-Filippino Lippi frescoes in the Brancacci Chapel of the Carmine, small groups of tourists wait uneasily, whispering; they try to find the lights for themselves; they try looking for someone in the sacristy. Finally a passing priest flicks on the electricity and hurries off, his robes flying. The same thing happens with the Ghirlandaio frescoes in Santa Trinita. Far from hovering, as the normal sacristan does, in ambush, waiting to expound the paintings, the Florentine sacristan does not make himself manifest until just before closing time, at midday, when he becomes very active, shooing people out of the church with shrill whistles and threatening gestures of his broom. If there are postcards for sale in a church, there is usually nobody to sell them.

This lack of co-operative spirit, this absence, this preoccupation, comes, after a time, and if you are not in a hurry, to seem one of the blessings of Florence, to make it, even, a hallowed place. This is one of the few cities where it is possible to loiter, undisturbed, in the churches, looking at the works of art. After the din outside, the churches are extraordinarily peaceful, so that you walk about on tiptoe, fearful of breaking the silence, of distracting the few old women, dimly seen, from their prayers. You can pass an hour, two hours, in the great churches of Brunelleschi – Santo Spirito and San Lorenzo – and no one will speak to you or pay you any heed. Touristic parties with guides do not penetrate here; they go instead to the Medici Chapels, to see the Michelangelos. The smaller churches – Santa Trinita, Santa Felicita, Ognissanti, Santissima Annunziata, Santa Maria Maddelena dei Pazzi, San Giovannino dei Cavalieri – are rarely visited; neither is the Pazzi Chapel in the Court of Santa Croce, and the wonderful Giottos, freshly restored, in the Bardi Chapel of Santa Croce, still surrounded by shaky scaffold, are seen only by art critics, their families and friends. San Miniato, on its hill, is too far away for most tourists; it is the church that, as they say, they missed. And the big churches of the preaching orders, Santa Maria Novella and Santa Croce, and the still bigger Duomo, where Savonarola delivered sermons to audiences of ten thousand, swallow up touristic parties, leaving hardly a trace. The tourists then complain of feeling 'dwarfed' by the architecture.

. . . As for the museums, they are the worst-organized, the worst-hung in Italy – a scandal, as the Florentines say themselves, with a certain civic pride. The exception, the new museum that has been opened in the old Fort of the Belvedere, with pale walls, wide views, cool rooms, sparsely hung, immediately became a subject of controversy, as did the new rooms of the Uffizi, which were held to be too white and uncluttered . . .

. . . Historic Florence is an incubus on its present population. It is like a vast piece of family property whose upkeep is too much for the heirs, who nevertheless find themselves criticized by strangers for letting the old place go to rack and ruin. History, in Venice, has been transmuted into legend; in Rome, the Eternal City, history is an everlasting present, an orderly perspective of arches receding from popes to Caesars with the papacy guaranteeing permanence and framing the vista of the future – decay being but an aspect of time's grandeur. If St Peter's were permitted to fall to pieces, it would still inspire awe, as the Forum does, while the dilapidation of Venetian palaces, reflected in lapping waters, is part of Venetian myth, celebrated already by Guardi and Belloto in the eighteenth century. Rome had Piranesi; Naples had Salvatore Rosa; but Florentine decay, in the Mercato Vecchio and the crooked byways of the Ghetto (now all destroyed and replaced by the Piazza della Repubblica), inspired only nineteenth-century water-colourists, whose work is preserved, not in art galleries, but in the topographical museum under the title of *Firenze Come Era* ('Florence as It Was'). History, for Florence, is neither a legend nor eternity, but a massive weight of rough building stone demanding continual repairs, pressing on the modern city like a debt, blocking progress.

Florence has always been a city of extremes, hot in the summer, cold in the winter, traditionally committed to advance, to modernism, yet containing backward elements narrow as its streets, cramped, stony, recalcitrant. It was the city where during the last war individual Fascists still held out fanatically after the city was taken by the Allies, and kept shooting as if for sport from the roof tops and loggias at citizens in the streets below. Throughout the Mussolini period, the Fascists in Florence had been the most violent and dangerous in Italy; at the same time, Florence had been the intellectual centre of anti-Fascism, and during the Resistance, the city as a whole 'redeemed itself' by a series of heroic exploits. The peasants of the *contado* showed a fantastic bravery in hiding enemies of the regime, and in the city many intellectuals and a few aristocrats risked their lives with great hardihood for the Resistance network. Florence, in short, was split, as it had always been, between the best and the worst. Even the Germans here were divided into two kinds. While the S.S. was torturing victims in a house on Via Bolognese (a nineteenth-century upper-middle class 'residential' district), across the city, on the old Piazza Santo Spirito, near Brunelleschi's church, the German Institute was hiding anti-Nazis in its library of reference works on Florentine art and culture. Such divisions, such extremism, such contrasts are *Firenze Come Era* – a terrible city, in many ways, uncomfortable and dangerous to live in, a city of drama, argument, and struggle.

From *The Stones of Florence*, MARY MCCARTHY

ARCO DI CIAMBELLA. PIAZZA DELLA MINERVA

Simple, erect, severe, austere, sublime –
Shrine of all saints and temple of all gods,
From Jove to Jesus – spared and bless'd by time,
Looking tranquillity, while falls or nods
Arch, empire, each thing round thee, and man plods
His way through thorns to ashes – glorious dome!
Shalt thou not last? Time's scythe and tyrant's rods
Shiver upon thee – sanctuary and home
Of art and piety – Pantheon! pride of Rome!

From *Childe Harold*, BYRON

ROME

Once upon a time, this city was a home to gods, now there's only Raphael in the Pantheon, a demigod, a darling of Apollo's, but the corpses that joined him later are a sorry bunch; a cardinal of dubious merit, a couple of monarchs and their purblind generals, high-flying civil servants, scholars that made it into the reference books, artists of academic distinction. Who gives a damn about them? The tour group stand in the ancient vaults, and gawp up at the light falling on them like rain through the only window, the circular opening in the cupola that was once covered with bronze tiles. Is it golden rain? Danaë succumbs to the approaches of Thomas Cook and the Italian Tourist Board; but without much enthusiasm. She won't lift her skirts to receive the god into her. Perseus won't be born. Medusa gets to keep her head and moves into a swish apartment. And what about great Jupiter? Is he here in our midst? Could he be the old fellow in the Amex office, or the rep for the German-European Travel agency? Or has he been banished to the edge of town somewhere, is he in the asylum enduring the questions of nosy psychiatrists, or languishing in the state's prisons? They've installed a she-wolf under the Capitol, a sick and depressed animal, not up to suckling Romulus and Remus. The faces of the tourists look pasty in the light of the Pantheon. Where is the baker that will knead them, where is the oven that will give them a bit of colour?

There is a trench going round the Pantheon that was once the street that led from the Temple of All the Gods to the Baths of

Agrippa; the Roman imperium collapsed, debris filled up the trench, archaeologists laid it bare again, masonry stumps rise up mossy and ruined, and sitting on top of them are the cats. There are cats all over Rome, they are the city's oldest inhabitants. A proud race like the Orsinis and the Colonnas, they are really the last true Romans, but they have fallen on hard times. Imperial names they have! Othello, Caligula, Nero, Tiberius. Children swarm round them, calling to them, taunting them. The voices of the children are loud and shrill, voluble, so appealing to a foreign ear. They lie on their fronts on the wall that runs alongside the ditch. School ribbons transform the grimy faces into little Renoirs. The girls' pinafores have ridden up, the boys wear tiny shorts, their legs look like those of statues under a patina of dust and sun. That's the beauty of Italy. Suddenly laughter rings out. They're laughing at an old woman. Compassion always has a pathetic aspect. The old woman hobbles along with a stick, bringing the cats something to eat. Something wrapped in a foul, sodden newspaper. Fishheads. On a blood-smeared newspaper photograph the American secretary of state and the Russian foreign minister are shaking hands. Myopic the pair of them. Their glasses blink. Thin lips compressed in a smile. The cats growl and hiss at each other. The old woman tosses the paper into the trench. Severed heads of sea-creatures, dull eyes, discoloured gills, opalescent scales, tumble among the yowling moggy mob. Carrion, a sharp whiff of excrement, secretions and sex, and the sweet smell of decay and purulence rise into the air, mixed with the exhaust fumes on the street, and the fresh, tempting aroma of coffee from the espresso bar on the corner of the Piazza della Rotonda. The cats fight over the leftovers. It's a

271

matter of life and death. Foolish creatures, why did they have to multiply! There are hundreds of them starving and homeless, randy, pregnant, cannibalistic; they are diseased and abandoned, and they have sunk about as far as cats can sink. One tom with a bullish skull, sulphur-yellow and bristle-haired, lords it over the weaker ones. He puts his paw down. He doles out. He takes for himself. His face bears the scars of past power struggles. He is missing part of an ear – a lost campaign. There is mange on his fur. The adoring children call him 'Benito'.

I was sitting at a zinc table, on a zinc chair, so light the wind might have carried me off. I was happy, I was telling myself, because I was in Rome, on the pavement terrace of an espresso bar on the corner of the Piazza della Rotonda in Rome, and I was drinking a brandy. The brandy also was light and flighty, light metal, like distilled zinc. It was grappa, and I was drinking it because I'd read in Hemingway that that's what you should drink in Italy. I wanted to be cheerful, but I didn't feel cheerful. Something was gnawing at me. Perhaps the awful mob of cats were gnawing me. No one likes seeing poverty, and a few pennies weren't enough to absolve you here. I never know what to do. I avert my eye. A lot of people do, but it bothers me. Hemingway doesn't seem to know the first thing about brandy. The grappa tasted mouldy and synthetic. It tasted like German black-market brandy from the Reichsmark period.

From *Death in Rome*, WOLFGANG KOEPPEN

Efix, the Pintor sisters' servant, had worked all day to shore up the primitive river embankment that he had slowly and laboriously built over the years. At nightfall he was contemplating his work from where he was sitting in front of his hut halfway up White Doves' Hill. A blue-green fringe of reeds rustled behind him.

Silently stretching out before him down to the river sparkling in the twilight was the little farm that Efix considers more his than the owners': thirty years of possession and work had certainly made it his, and the two hedgerows of prickly pear that enclose it like two gray walls meandering from terrace to terrace, from the hill to the river, are like the boundaries of the world to him.

In his survey the servant ignored the land on either side of the farm because it had once been Pintor property. Why dredge up the past? Useless regret. Better to think about the future and hope in God's help.

And God promised a good year, or at least He had covered all the almond and peach trees in the valley with blossoms; and this valley, between two rows of white hills covered with spring vegetation, water, scrub, flowers, together with the distant blue mountains to the west and the blue sea to the east, gave the impression of a cradle billowing with green veils and blue ribbons, with the river murmuring monotonously like a sleepy child.

But the days were already too hot and Efix was also thinking about the torrential rains that swell the bankless river and make it leap like an all-destroying monster. One could hope, but had to be watchful, like the reeds along the riverbank beating their leaves together with every breath of wind as though warning of danger.

That was why he had worked all day and now, waiting for night, he wove a reed mat so as not to waste time and prayed that God make his work worthwhile. What good is a little embankment if God's will doesn't make it as formidable as a mountain?

Seven reeds across a willow twig, and seven prayers to the Lord and to Our Lady of Rimedio, bless her. In the intense twilight blue her little church and the quiet circle of cabins around it down below lay like a centuries-old abandoned prehistoric village. At this hour, as the moon bloomed like a big rose in the bushes on the hill and euphorbia spread its perfume along the river, Efix's mistresses were also praying. Donna Ester, the oldest, bless her, was certainly remembering him, the sinner. This was enough to make him feel happy, compensated for his efforts.

Footsteps in the distance made him look up. They sounded familiar. It was the light, swift stride of a boy, the stride of an angel hurrying with some happy or sad announcement. God's will be done. It's He who sends good and bad news; but Efix's heart began to pound, and his black cracked fingers trembled on the silvery reeds shining in the moonlight like threads of water.

The footsteps were no longer heard. Nevertheless, Efix remained motionless, waiting.

The moon rose before him, and evening voices told him the day had ended: a cuckoo's rhythmical cry, the early crickets' chirping, a bird calling; the reeds sighing and the ever more distinct voice of the river; but most of all a breathing, a mysterious panting that seemed to come from the earth itself. Yes, man's working day was done, but the fantastic life of elves, fairies, wandering spirits was beginning. Ghosts of the ancient Barons came down from the Castle ruins above Galte on Efix's left and ran along the river hunting wild boar and fox. Their guns gleamed in the short alder trees along the riverbed, and the faint sound of barking dogs in the distance was a sign of their passing.

Efix could hear the sound that the *panas* – women who died in childbirth – made while washing their clothes down by the river, beating them with a dead man's shin bone, and he believed he saw the *ammattadore* (the elf with seven caps where he hid his treasure) jumping about under the almond woods, followed by vampires with steel tails.

It was the elf that caused the branches and rocks to glitter under the moon. And along with the evil spirits were spirits of unbaptized babies – white spirits that flew through the air changing themselves into little silvery clouds behind the moon. And dwarfs and *janas* – the little fairies who stay in their small rock houses during the day weaving gold cloth on their golden looms – were dancing in the large phillyrea bushes, while giants looked out from the rocks on the moonstruck mountains, holding the bridles of enormous horses that only they can mount, squinting to see if down there within the expanse of evil euphorbia a dragon was lurking. Or if the legendary *cananéa*, living from the time of Christ, was slithering around on the sandy marshland.

During moonlit nights especially this entire mysterious population animates the hills and valleys. Man has no right to disturb it with his presence, just as the spirits have respected him during the sun's course; therefore it's time to retire and close one's eyes under the protection of guardian angels.

Efix made the sign of the cross and stood up, but he was still waiting for someone. Nevertheless he shoved the plank that served as a door across the entry way and leaned a big reed cross against it to keep spirits and temptation from entering his hut.

Through the cracks the moonlight illuminated the corners of the low, narrow room – but a room large enough for someone like him who was as small and scrawny as a young boy. From the conical cane and reed roof over the dry stone walls, with a hole in the middle for the smoke to escape, hung bunches of onions and dry herbs, palm crosses and blessed olive branches, a painted candle, a scythe for keeping vampires away, and a little sack of barley for protection against the *panas*. With every breath of air everything quivered and spider webs shone in the moonlight. On the floor a two-handled pitcher lay on its side, and a pan rested upside down next to it.

Efix unrolled his mat but didn't lie down. He thought he kept hearing the sound of a boy's footsteps. Someone was certainly coming, and in fact dogs on nearby farms suddenly began to bark, and the whole countryside, which a few moments earlier seemed to sleep amid prayers murmured by nocturnal voices, was full of echoes and rustling almost as though it had suddenly jerked awake.

Efix pushed the plank aside. A black figure was coming over the rise where the low bean plants grew silvery under the moonlight, and he, to whom even human shapes seemed mysterious at night, made the sign of the cross again. But a voice he recognized called out to him. It was the clear but slightly breathless voice of the boy who lived next door to the Pintor sisters.

'Zio Efisé, Zio Efisé!'

From *Reeds in the Wind*, GRAZIA DELEDDA